Whispers of a Missionary:
True Stories From the Mission Field

I

By

Isaac Abladesa

Dedication

To all those who have given up their lives for the sake of evangelism....

To those who possess burning hearts to accomplish the last command of Jesus Christ....

To those who bow their knees for the sake of evangelism...

To those men and women who have been neglected in the forests, mountains, and wilderness to carry out the Gospel of salvation to the unsaved....

I dedicate this book.

Perhaps it will kindle the hearts of many to walk down this path, giving others the way to salvation.

G.A

Acknowledgments

I would like to thank my Lord Jesus, my Savior who allowed me to pass through this wonderful experience and helped me to put them into word so that I may share them with others.

I would like to acknowledge the support of my wonderful wife Nermeen for bearing the long hours as a worked on this book

I would also like to thank Dena Beshai for her help in editing Whispers of a Missionary.

Lastly I would like to thank my nephew Matthew Masoud for assisting me in translating this book

My God Bless their works

Contents

Introduction

This book, my beloved reader, contains true stories that occurred during my missionary travels. A majority occurred in Zambia while some occurred in Egypt. These stories depict God's work and His mighty hand in the salvation of others. He utilized us, the missionaries--His weak vessels, to aid in that salvation.

While sharing these stories in church meetings, my companions suggested I write a book. I chose the title *Whispers of a Missionary* because my grandmother would whisper stories to me when I was young and I still remember a majority of these stories. In the clamor of this crazy life, I want to whisper these stories in your ear.. I suggest putting this book on your nightstand and reading a story every night.

I wish from all my heart that these whispers become loud voice that will invite you to join in the evangelical work. Christ will utilize you to save others.

God bless you.

Part I

Ministry in Africa

Divine Care

Our God is a God of miracles. Several miracles occurred daily in the mission field. These miracles have demonstrated God's mighty hand and care for us. These miracles deliver a clear message from God that tells us, "Don't worry, everything is under My control". We learned, from God's daily dealings with us, to put all our yuck and needs upon Him, and also to trust in Him blindly and obey Him in all that He asks us to do without condition or restriction, and even sometimes without understanding. As David the prophet says "I was so foolish and ignorant; I was like a beast before you." (Psalm 73:22)

These miracles are the fuel that kindles our faith and allows us to trust in Him until it becomes our way of life.

One particular story begins when we were on our way to a rural area, which we visited once a month. This area had a church which, to say, is still under "spiritual construction." Only 20 people had been baptized and the rest of the attendance of our meetings were residents from the area, and non-believers that had not joined our church yet but enjoyed attending our meetings. This area, called Mazabuka, was about 80 miles south of the mission station in the capital city Lusaka, Zambia. When we embarked to this particular ministry, we prepared everything from food to the Sunday School materials, even brought the pews with us because in Mazabuka, there was nothing. We loaded the pickup with all our needs for the services of that day. Usually we began very early in the morning because the drive took about an hour and a half, and that way, we could arrive early to spend as long as possible in the service and still return before dark.

One day while we were going and had already made it half way, I discovered I did not have enough fuel to return as the fuel gage was almost on zero. I knew that there were some gas stations on the road where we could fuel up and rest if needed. But then I remembered I did not have any money with me. I had forgotten to get money before I left. When I asked the servants with me, all Zambians, if they had any money, all answered negatively. I had two options, either to go back to the mission station to get money to then go back to Mazabuka, or to go to the service as planned and try to finish before sunset and return and wherever we would stop, we would call someone to either bring us money or fuel. In the first case, we would have wasted a large amount of time and we would have been late, especially because the people would be waiting for us in the mud church, already singing. I offered and discussed the two solutions with the servants with me; all of us chose the second solution; to go to the ministry and God would provide a way back. In Africa, one does not pay for fuel by credit card or visa, and there is no insurance company like AAA to tow for us. On the mission field, you just have to place your trust in God.

We arrived to Mazabuka on time and we tried as much as we could to leave before it became dark. We did not cancel anything from the ministry program. Both us and the people were very joyful and had forgot about the money and fuel problem. When we began our return trip at around 5:00 in the evening, I looked at the fuel gage and it was exactly at zero. I told the servants we would begin the trip, drive the car until it stopped, and then figure out what to do next. Our options then would be to either call someone from the mission station or ask for nearby help. We spent the first 10 miles without any problems. Every second, we expected the car to stop. I increased my speed in order to decrease the gap between our location and the mission station. Expecting the fuel to run out at any moment, we were surprised when that never happened. All the people with me stared in wonder at how the fuel gage was at zero on the whole return trip, but the car never stopped. But the surprise and real miracle is that we arrived to the mission station in Lusaka without any problems.

It was very clear God's work and His mighty hands. It was a miracle by all means. When I went to get fuel, I found the fuel gage fully functioning. Unfaithfully, I told myself that maybe the fuel gage was not working. But I knew in my heart that God's work and care is what kept us without delay. Doesn't he say that, *"Take nothing for the journey, neither staffs nor bag nor bread nor money; and do not have two tunics apiece."(Luke 9:3)*

Tree of Life

When God chased Adam out of the Garden of Eden after he ate from the tree of knowledge of good and evil, He assigned one of the Cherubim, with a fire sword in his hand, to protect the tree of life and prevent Adam from eating from it and living in sin forever. This is the first we hear of the tree of life (Genesis3). It is very clear from its name it is a tree to provide life, and contain life in its branches. However, I'm mentioning a different type of "Tree of Life". A tree that carries death in its roots and receives nutrition from other people's life. Even though it's called Tree of Life, its name does not indicate how this tree germinated and grew.

The Mano tribe is a small tribe of approximately three hundred and twenty thousand people distributed in the western part of Africa. Few of them live southeast of the Guinea Republic. The Mano tribe believes in many traditions and customs that, to us, are considered myths. Myths that must be eradicated. Unfortunately, they believe their tradition and customs are the secret for their current existence. Here I am in the process of describing one of the strongest Mano traditions, without it, they would be condemned to their cessation of being. Because, simply they believe this tradition is the cause for their growth and survival which is the tree of life.

The Mano tribe lives in scattered villages. Each village is made up of a few hundred people or less. They depend on horizontal expansion, meaning, they do not increase the number of villagers. Instead, if a village becomes overpopulated, some families must break off from the main village and start a new one. They live in bushes and work as sheep grazers.

The Mano is considered an un-targetable tribe for evangelism. The number of Christians in the tribe are a couple hundred and still keep some of their cultural traditions. The Mano language is not written. A Bible translations ministry, only about thirty years ago, began to make Mano a written language instead of just an oral language and to translate the Holy Bible. They translated the four gospels and the book of Acts. The missionaries are still working to finish the New Testament.

I met one of those missionaries. She specialized in linguistics, and had come recently to the Mano tribe to help complete the translation of the New Testament to their language and to deliver the salvation message to the Mano tribe. She spoke to me about the Mano tribe's strange traditions; one of them is about how they begin a new village.

When a village begins to become over populated, some of the families decide to separate to a new place. A group of them go on a search to where they can establish a new village. After they find a suitable place, a male member of one of the families goes to this new place and brings with him a newborn child. This child was given to him voluntarily by another family. The man then goes with the child to the new place, and buries the child alive, along with some seeds, and vows to water and sow the seeds until it begins to germinate. They call this new tree, the "Tree of Life." After the tree begins to grow, the families may now move to the new village. They call it the tree of life because the tree derived from the life of the newborn child. The tree is respected and honored by all in the village. They also treat this tree almost up to a level of worshiping it. Therefore, the sacrifice of a child's life was given for the continuation of the tribe's existence. Thus, death has become a source of new life.

I was really astonished at how some tribes were still living by these traditions in the twenty first century. How desperate the need was for the Mano tribe to know the true source of life, Jesus Christ! How desperate were they to know that Jesus was buried and with him buried the seed of sin, so that we can become living branches in His vine so we could live forever.

Guinea, Conakry 2005

Maya Maya Tribe

I am often invited to share my stories about the mission in Africa. One question always seems to repeat itself, "Is there really cannibalism in Africa?" My definite answer is that now there is no cannibalism anywhere. My answer is not built on sure knowledge and research. But it is a result of my inner self refusing to believe such actions occur. Personally, I had never heard about any cannibalism. I heard about people that eat monkeys, camels, and zebras-- but never humans. I maintained this belief until I went to the Congo in mid-August 2004.

The Congo is considered one of the richest countries in Africa in natural resources. However, the Congo is one of the poorest and most miserable countries in the world, a result of civil war between tribes and opposition to the government. During my 2004 visit, there was a vicious war in different parts of the country. One incident in particular, was very brutal.

They Maya Maya tribe mostly reside in the Kananga province. The members of the Maya Maya tribe live strictly in the jungle and forest. They believe in many demonic rituals. At the center of their traditions, is the drinking of human blood. The tribe believes that drinking human blood will grant them a long life and eating human flesh will give them superhuman strength. This superhuman strength will grant them strength even against death. However, they do not eat each other. They eat only the people who betray them or outsiders.

A few days before our arrival, two Congolese Catholic priests came to evangelize the Maya Maya tribe in an attempt to turn them from their horrid ways. After they had stayed with them for a period of time, the chief and committee of the tribe asked them to leave and warned them if they did not leave they would be eaten. The two fathers did not care about the threats and continued to preach to them the Gospel in order to change their ways. Shortly after the chief and committee's warning, the two fathers were found killed. Certain parts such as the muscles were missing from their corpses. Despite the intervention of the Vatican and Congolese army, they were not able to catch the people responsible for this tragedy because they live very deep in the bush and jungle areas. This event happened only three days before our arrival and this event was all the public and media could speak of.

Now my beloved reader, do you now know the answer to whether or not cannibalism still exists around the world? I ask of you now to raise your heart in prayer for the Maya Maya tribe and all tribes still in the depths of the darkness, ignorance, and sin.

Love More

His name was Love More. I was frequently heard his name come up in the mission station, but I never met him. I only heard about him. I was just expecting him to be one of hundreds of thousands in Zambia and different countries in Africa who suffer from hunger, endemic disease, poverty, and seek the basic need for subsistence.

One day I was passing in front of the mission clinic and I met a church member that asked me to give a recommendation letter for a doctor to examine Love More. Love More was short, shaggy haired, and had a slight hunch back. It seemed as if his head was placed between his shoulders and had an oblate nose like most of the African people. He had thin lips. Because of his scrawny stature, he was groggy on his feet. His clothes were ragged. Although he tried to fit his worn clothing, he failed desperately. His shoes were torn to the point that he converted them into slippers. Slippers that were so badly torn they no longer served their function. His eyes were pale and clearly demonstrated his nearby death. You could never have guessed his actual age of thirty-six.

I knew from first sight he was suffering from the symptoms of HIV. At this point there was no hope for him to get well. Later I found out he stayed alone with no relatives. He was alone in the capital city Lusaka.

He more frequently began coming to the church asking for his subsistence needs. The subsistence needs for any western dog or cat exceeds the needs of Love More. There is no one to help him up. He did not care much of what he ate, wore, or slept. What he needed the most was more love for a person that knew his days were numbered. At times it seemed he was doing fine and he was getting better, stronger. But then his illness would act up again and he would return to the previous state.

After a while the father in charge baptized him and began giving him the Eucharist. Although he was getting medication and ARVs (HIV Treatment), he had no improvement. When the illness was at its peak, he stopped coming to church. It was usual for the priest to take the Eucharist to the homes of sick people. The father told me before Wednesday liturgy he would give communion to some of the sick people and that I should join him. Love More was among those people.

The trip to where Love More lived was difficult because he lived in a poverty-stricken area. When we arrived he was waiting to receive us with a big simple smile. Love More's facial hair began to thicken because he could not afford for someone to shave his face nor did he have the health to shave himself. We sat on the street and the priest gave him the Holy Communion.

I was curious to know where he lived and slept. My curiosity led me to a one-foot hole under the ground that was about five feet by six feet. Love More had flattened out metal barrels and had used them as walls and ceiling. I asked one of his neighbors if he sleeps here and she answered affirmatively. I looked without entering and noticed on my right hand wooden beams. Four wooden sticks were engraved in the mud met by wooden beams that had cardboard layers on top. That was Love More's bed. In this room, which was much more of a hole, there was string that ran across the top of the room and rag clothes hung on it containing a stench. In the back, there were cardboard boxes. The only light in this hole was the holes in the ceiling. I asked his neighbor what he does during rainy season. Does the water come in and flood his home? She told me that they create a small canal to escort the water outside the house (the hole). I pointed at the holes on the ceiling and walls and I asked, "What about these?" She did not answer. My curiosity led me to ask about his daily meals and daily needs. She told me everyone helps with that.

We left the place to visit other sick people and give them Holy Communion. After a few days, I left Zambia but Love More did not leave me, my mind, or my daily dreams. I was asking myself how many people like Love More need more love and better care. I would hear His voice powerfully *"for I was hungry and you gave Me food; I was thirsty and you gave Me drink; I was a stranger and you took Me in;* [36] *I was naked and you clothed Me; I was sick and you visited Me; I was in prison and you came to Me"* *(Matthew25:35).*

After a while I came back to Zambia and asked about Love More. I was told he went back to his village in the bushes. It is customary to return to one's village when one is very ill and preparing for death. Love More never came back from his village, but he came back to live with me in my heart to establish a hospice for all those like Love More.

Immanuel

It was mid-December, 10:00 pm and the place Lusaka, the capital of Zambia, specifically at the North mead neighborhood.

This time of year is the peak of the rainy season. Usually it rains continuously for days. Torrents interrupt normal rain. These torrential rains leave behind flooded streets for a few hours until it enters the drains. After the torrents, normal showers return.

Signs of Christmas celebrations are everywhere. Santa Claus in the shopping centers, big Christmas trees in the city squares, Christmas lights surround the houses. Christmas vacation advertisements increase drastically during this time. Even the schools close for a few weeks. The invitations between friends increase. Many friends gather together in a home to sing Christmas carols, eat Christmas cookies, and drink warm wine with cinnamon. This is an English tradition that many of the English people in Zambia still do. Grants and donations increase extraordinarily at the same time beggars, street kids, and hijackers increase just as much. Most of the missionaries working in churches take their vacations after the New Year because this is the time they are the busiest raising funds, celebrating, and receiving invitations.

A little after 10:00 in the evening, I was returning home from visiting some of my missionary friends. Everything was calm after a very heavy rain. Still some light drops were present indicating the rain had not yet regressed. While I drove, I talked to Him. "*What would you like me to offer to You this year?' 'What will my gift be compared to Your gift, your Son.?"*

I saw a traffic light turned, so I slowed down and stopped. I witnessed on my right side a nearly naked child standing next to my vehicle. I looked at him; he had a slim body and was about thirteen years old. His cheek and collar bones were clearly visible as a result of malnutrition, his feet bare. He had little protruding eyes with humble features. His clothes were torn to the point I considered naked. He had brought his finger up to his mouth signaling he was hungry. I opened the window although I knew that was very dangerous because many hijacking happen this way. When I opened the window he began saying,
"Bouana enjala maningy coliba maqudia bouna" which means "Sir, I am very hungry. I don't have food sir" He continued "Coliba mandalama" which means I have no money. I waited until he finished then I asked him in his local language, what his name was. He answered "Immanuel." I asked him where he lived and he answered me in Chaisa. Chaisa is about four miles from the North Mead area, where we were. I asked him again, "what do you want?" He answered; I need money to buy food. I told him, I can't give you money because I do not have money. He begged and said "nababata buana," which means "please sir." The traffic light was about to turn green so I asked him to jump inside the car. After he did, I turned left to the mission station in Manchinchi Road in the North Mead area.

Everything was very quiet in the mission station. It was quite late. I took Immanuel to the guest house and prepared for him a meal. He was eating with concerned eyes looking right and left. He was not used to eating on a table, with a spoon or fork. He was eating quickly too.

"Did you like the food," I asked him.

"Maningi Buana," meaning, yes, so much, answered Immanuel.

He ate fast and did not even finish half of the plate I prepared for him. I asked him why he had not finished his food, he had answered he was full. Later I figured why this was. Because of Immanuel's lack of food, his stomach shrunk and therefore any small amount of food would fill him. I asked him, "How many friends do you have with you?" as I know the street kids do not stay alone.

"Four," he answered. I prepared a food basket enough for four and I gave it to him saying, "This is for you and your friends and you may come to me if you are hungry."

A few days later, I met Immanuel at one of the gas stations in the area. He came close to me and said "Mr. Isaac do you remember me?" I looked towards the voice and he reminded me his name and showed me his friends who were with him. I asked him why he didn't come again for food. He did not answer.

We followed Immanuel and his friends. We figured out they are orphans who were victims of HIV parents. They died and left them without any guardians. We were unsure of what actions we should take with Immanuel and his friends. We had no orphanage to accommodate them. The ideal solution was to go to their relatives; aunts, uncles, whoever was available and asked them to house the children; we would take care of all the other needs such as food, clothes, soap, groceries, and even school fees. This was mean to take them away from the streets and to prevent gangs from recruiting them for hijacking, stealing, and sometimes even killing.

The average life expectancy for men in Zambia is 37 years. The women's life expectancy only increases by 7 months. This is the result of the prevalence of HIV in Zambia which affects about 36% of the population. As a result, 10% of the total population are orphans, numbering about 1,000,000.

Our mission is now taking care of more than 200 children in Zambia and Kenya. Every child cost about thirty dollars a month to accommodate.

One of the tribes' headmen, Mr. Mauni, gave us a piece of land to build a school and orphanage for these kids in addition to some land to cultivate in order to support them. We are praying to God to put this project in action.

Bare Footed

One day in June, 2001, I was going to Zambia by road from Johannesburg, South Africa. I stopped a few days in Zimbabwe to visit our mission there. It was bitterly cold and the trip by bus was not easy. It was over a fifteen-hour trip, with rest.

After I arrived to the capital, Harare, I began with my service with the father in visitation. Next day the service was scheduled at two o'clock in the afternoon to visit a new area under "spiritual construction." It was about eight miles south from the mission station in Harare. We found everyone ready, singing spiritual songs, very cheerful, and praising unceasingly. As soon as they saw us they heightened in singing and praise, playing the drums strongly. The joy and jubilation permeated the place. Everyone was sitting on the floor in a hall made of tinplate and wood. The hall had a length of about 20 feet and a width of about 12 feet. The roof was thatched as most African huts are.

After prayer, the father introduced me and I gave a small sermon about God's love for us. After we finished, the father distributed some donations in kind. On our way back, the father told me how the service started in this area. One of the church members moved to the area. She started to tell her neighborhood about the church. After a while she asked the father to come meet the people over there. Time went on and the lady donated part of her house to be the church. After a few months of regular weekly visitations, the father baptized those who had accepted the faith and wanted to join the church. Every month he would pray for them a liturgy and would give them the Eucharist.

The father was supposed to leave Zimbabwe after a few days. This was the last Sunday before he would leave for his annual vacation. On this specific Sunday, he gathered all the congregations of the churches he served in to pray one liturgy in the mission station at Harare. The father had arranged for their transportation.

The liturgy was supposed to start at 10 am so that all the congregations would have an opportunity to arrive at the mission station on time and so the weather would have a chance to warm up. At 7:00 AM, we were surprised by strong knocking on the church gate. I did not know what I was supposed to do. Was I supposed to see who was knocking or should I go speak to the father. My confusion did not last long because I saw the father leave his house to go see who was knocking. I changed my clothes quickly to go after him. The temperature was freezing. There was snow on the floor. When I followed the father to go see who was at the gate, I found him with a tall, elderly man, who was strong of stature. They were talking. When I came closer, I guessed his age to be in his mid-fifties. After I greeted him, he left us and walked towards the church. The father told me he was from the new area where I gave the sermon the day before. The elderly man did not wait to come with the rest of the congregation by bus. He preferred to come early to the church. He kept telling the father, "I am so proud to be the first one to come to the church." He walked about eight miles in freezing conditions for more than two hours just because he was eager to come early to church and was not patient enough to wait to come with the rest of the congregation by bus.

Then the father asked me "Do you know what I am wondering about him?" I looked to him curiously. He answered "He is barefoot." I looked to the man to find he was truly barefoot, walking with his strong and tall stature, toward the church, indifferent about the weather and the length of his trip.

While I do not know his name, he brought me a silent message about our complacency to go to church early. How we have the luxury and our climate-controlled cars. The church, just a few minutes driving and our laziness still preventing us from going early. I have no doubt this man will stand at the last day to condemn us, as Jesus said about the people of Nineveh, how they will condemn His generation. How many of the new believers, those who recently accepted Jesus are more active and inflamed than those who are born as Christians.

God Whom I Believe In

I was flying from Johannesburg to Amsterdam on my way to the United States in August 2003. It was a cold night and the trip took about ten hours. The Boeing plane was very crowded. Before boarding, I spoke with a South African woman, Jackie originally from Holland. She had immigrated a few decades ago to South Africa. She was reading the Bible. We chatted about the world's need for Christ. When we boarded the plane, Jackie sat not too far from me. Next to me sat two women in their mid-fifties. It did not take long before we introduced each other. They were South African and on their way to Norway. They were worked for an adoption organization. They would take the children who were born on the streets and adopt them to families around the world. The woman next to me, Brittney was Caucasian, owl faced with minute features. She had brown, short hair and her eyes were blue. She was well-dressed and had polite manners and humble expressions.

She told me she was atheist. She did not believe God exists but she claimed she did not do wrong. Hypothetically, she said, if there was a god, she would not need him. She was speaking very politely. I tried to explain the exact order of the universe, the human body, and creatures. All this couldn't exist accidently. The chance of the universe being created accidently is zero and if she doesn't need Him, He needs her. At this point she asked me, "What would He need me for." To be with you and enjoy talking with you as he said *"And my delight was with the sons of men" (Proverbs 8:31)*. I felt as though she had a false image of God. So I asked her "What are the characteristics of God that you do not believe in?"

She talked a lot about God controlling people, judging them, and sending them to hell if they do evil. If God existed, then why would there be so much pain suffering and evil in the world. Why is He silent about what's happening. I answered her that the god you are talking about and refuse to believe in, I refuse to believe in, too. My God is different.

Truly as Pope Maximus IV said, "the god the atheists refuse to believe in, I refuse to believe in him, too." God's image which Marx, Sartre, and Kant had envisioned and refused is a god I refuse, also. However, many believers' ideas about the god whom they worship makes me not believe in their god. The god who is refused and not accepted by the atheist does not exist.

I began to think about the God whom I believe and know. The God that maybe this woman does not know. I have read an article by Father Juan Arias and God does not believe in and I have found in the contrary of this characters my God. I want you to know my God. If you haven't known him before, you can share my knowledge about him. You will find him different.

My God does not denounce materialistic things.

My God can easily answer the problems that face man.

My God can easily deal with an honest man coming to him and proclaiming, "I can't".

My God does not like suffering and does not place it upon man.

My God does not object to people's happiness.

My God does not give us happiness we do not understand.

My God does not work without man and respects his will.

My God runs after those who stray from him.

My God can forgive what other people judge.

My God does not bring evil to man but everything he gives is His blessings.

My God does not enjoy war but He is the Prince of Peace.

My God is not a referee that plays and controls the rules.

My God does not impose terror in man's heart.

My God is pleased when we communicate with Him informally.

My God cannot be monopolized by any group, church, culture, or religion.

My God smiles at human tricks and deceptions.

My God gives hope to man and does not send them to hellfire but prepares for them an eternal paradise.

My God does not ask for what is beyond our human capabilities and he knows our humanity will fail many times before it succeeds.

My God cannot be explained by philosophy or science.

My God's delight is with the sons of men.

My God, if you believe in Him will not ask you to waiver from what makes you human.

My God is understood by children and the simple people more than the wise and intelligent.

My God you cannot love unless you love others.

My God does not denounce sex but sanctifies it.

My God does not regret what He gives man, even freedom to reject and insult him.

My God helps man to grow and develop until he reaches His image.

My God becomes emotional in the presence of a crying person or smiling child.

My God is everywhere, not only at the churches, prayer meeting, or sermons.

My God can be found in a child's eye, weeping mother, persecuted person.

My God never combines with politics.

My God will declare himself if you ask sincerely to know Him.

My God loves what is rejected and hated by many.

My God does not prefer the strong over the weak, or the rich over the poor.

My God has a very unique way to deal with every individual.

My God did not establish a static church, but a dynamic church able to develop and to better itself.

My God allows us to grow our conscience above the law.

My God you cannot be close to if you gossip with your neighbor and condemn others.

My God will never say to you, "You will pay the price."

My God will never accept you if you do not work but praise him the whole day.

My God is very reactive to people's problems and their pain.

My God gives like the sun, does not differentiate between the flower and the dung.

My God gives us a paradise that we will all be brothers and sisters and the source of light will be the love that fills all of us.

My God, it is not necessary to talk to Him bowing but he needs your heart in prayer.

My God, you may not always understand His will, but trust He does what is best for you.

My God understands that as children we can forget and get dirty, too.

My God does not get bored from forgiving a person that comes to him saying, "I'm Sorry."

My God's priests and servants do not have answers to every question, sometimes the answer is, "We do not know."

My God is more concerned about love and mercy more than fasting and worshipping.

My God loves you with your weakness and gives you the power to change.

My God if you touch Him, you will never be concerned about anybody else.

My God no matter how much you try to know Him, you will never be able to truly comprehend Him.

My God can make everything new.

My God is not a god of priests that think they are above sin or have divine right.

My God is not a god of priests that preach that hell is full of people, and heaven is almost empty.

My God knows the way to the people's pain, what makes them sad, and he wept with them.

My God powerfully came to the earth and was born a man.

My God saved man from his sins.

My God is love. Where He is you will find love.

Really, what an awesome God.

Before I left the plane I looked for the bible to give to Brittany, but I did not find with me an English version. So I went to Jackie and I asked for her bible. I told her the reason. She gave it to me joyfully and then I gave it to Brittany. She promised she would read it to know my God as I explained Him to her.

Mr. Coni

One of my most favorite services is to visit the prisons. Prisons have a bizarre variety of people. Many of them, from their perspective, are innocent. To them, they did nothing worthy of being punished in prison. They think the true criminal and thieves are outside the walls of the prison. But for them it was just unfortunate luck that led them to this fate. Hearing this, I smiled, leading them to believe that I believed them. The issue in Zambia is completely different. After being arrested you are sent to prison until the time of your trial. Because of the low number of judges and few slow courts, your case may take a few years to be seen. You might be declared innocent and be set free to start your life over, after losing everything while you were behind the prison wall. Guilty until proven innocent, not vice versa.

In the Lusaka prison, what is really strange is one-third of the prisoners are from different nationalities that had problems with immigration. The system places you in prison until you are able to pay a penalty, which most can't pay because it is too high. Or they will expel you from the country which takes a few years to happen. Most die inside the prison. Their embassies do not take care of them, especially with the poor countries.

The prison's capacity is designed for four hundred people only. In best case scenario the number is no less than thirteen hundred. The cell is designed for forty people.

Sometimes there are ninety or a hundred people. There are no lights, air vents, or windows. Each individual would sit and open his leg then another person would sit in between his legs and so on, creating long chains from wall to wall. The whole night up to seven in the morning in this arrangement.

Scabies and pneumonia are very common among the prisoners. They usually isolate the sick in one or two cells depending on the number, until they die. Whoever can overcome the illness returns back to the healthy cells. Many times we distribute drugs for scabies and many other diseases. The problem with pneumonia is not just the drugs, but also the ventilation and nutrition. Both are not available in the prison. The men that do not receive food from their families suffer from starvation. Usually the prisoners swap the food they get for things such as protection, clothes, and cigarettes.

One day, I went to our weekly meeting, but I found all the prisoners in complete chaos. They were standing in long lines. I asked the reason for the chaos. I was told that today there was breakfast (porridge). Corn flour, mixed with boiled water and some salt. They apologized that they will not be able to have a meeting because there was breakfast. Their excuse is that we have a meeting every week, but we do not get breakfast.

Sodomy is very common in prison. If you want to prevent being attacked you need to be under the banner of a strong man, but you have to pay him.

When a prisoner gets sick, they take him to the hospital but he receives no treatment. The maximum that could be done is to examine him, write a prescription and return him back to the prison. When I asked why they do not hospitalize him or give him medication, I was told there wasn't enough room in the hospitals for all. So they choose to treat a good citizen over the prisoner.

The prison is a big circular arena. The diameter is over one hundred feet. The cells are on the perimeter of the arena. There is a small library for the prisoner, open during the day. I found some books written by our church authors. To the right of the library, there is a long line of showers, without dividers. The prisoners shower completely naked. The prisoners use a small area between the showers and library as a barber place. In the prison I met many African nationalities such as Sudanese, Congolese, Ethiopian, Cameroonian, Some Asians and two Europeans. Many times we helped those prisoners that have problems with immigration. To pay the penalty and deport them back to their countries. The largest number we helped at one time was a group of Ethiopians. They were nine people. As I was finishing the paperwork, the prison warden asked "Who is responsible for helping these people to be released at one time?" They told him about me. He stared at me for quite a long time before he signed the paper. I assume the stare was a result of the large penalty bill.

One day, I met a couple from China. I thought they were married and the women was visiting her husband. After a while I found a guard guiding the women to the women's prison. I was told they were in need of help. For me, this was a good window of opportunity to evangelize to them.

For a long time I was concerned about evangelizing to the Chinese. Like the majority of the Chinese people, this couple did not speak English or any other language. I found a Zambian prisoner that spoke some Mandarin. He helped me communicate with them. I understood from his interpretation that they have a problem with immigration. I asked the Zambian prisoner to translate. I began to tell them about a God that has the upper hand and controls everything. He planned their coming to Zambia in the prison so that I may tell them about His love. The man pulled out from under his shirt, a big cross. He told me in

Mandarin, he is Catholic. They escaped from the persecution in China and came to Zambia with a Japanese passport. Later, I understood the Japanese do not need a visa to get in Zambia. So they can escape to England and file for asylum. After that, they can send to their families to come to join them.

During the transit in Zambia, because they carried Japanese passports, they brought them a Japanese interpreter. Here they discovered they were not Japanese and got caught. After hearing their story, I went to the Chinese embassy a few times, but I failed to meet anyone. Only once they spoke to me through the phone. They told me they would do their best to get them out and send them back to China. I went to the immigration and tried to pay the penalty. The problem was greater than just a penalty –it was fraud. What I could do was visit them regularly and give them food. One day I went to visit them. I found out they were deported back to China. The women left a letter for me with her mailing address. I never got a reply from her.

I visited the prison every Thursday. The service was from nine to ten thirty in the morning. I always find them in a state of readiness. All the prisoners are gathered in the arena in three groups. One on the right, one on the left, and one on the middle. Even the sick were carried outside the cell for the service. Most of the work was stopped. A building at the head of the arena was by far the tallest. They placed the podium on the front of the building, for shade. There was no microphone, so the speaker must make his voice very loud, so all 1400 attendees could hear. There was a choir from every cell. Every choir rotated in singing before the service. After the songs we prayed, gave a sermon, and closed with a prayer meeting. After we finished the service, many prisoners came to us with their requests. Some needed medication, others needed to contact their families and relatives, and some needed to just talk.

Many times we distributed clothes and food. Usually, we would spend over two hours after the service for those matters. For weeks we distributed clothes, as there were many naked prisoners that had spent a long time in the prison and no one had asked about them. We gave those naked people more clothes. After a few weeks I found they were naked again. When I asked, I was told they traded the clothes we gave them with food.

One day, after I finished my speech, three men came to me separately. All three of them asked to become Christian and to be baptized. One from Cameroon, one from Sri Lanka, and the third from Zambia. The one from Cameroon was Buddhist, but his family was Christian. He became a Buddhist long ago. He spoke poor English. My French at the time was not good. The communication between us was difficult. Although hard, our conversation was interesting and enjoyable. The man was very slim, tall, and owned nothing more than what he had on. His face was oval with a light mustache. He had tan skin and a long forehead. He spoke slowly as he told me how he got arrested. He exceeded his stay in Zambia and could not afford to pay the penalty. He was trying to reach his family to pay the penalty. I got his family's number and tried to call them, but in vain.

The man from Sri Lanka was Buddhist, too. He had the same problem with immigration. Medium height, broad shoulders and a strong structure. He had a heavy mustache, with dark straight hair, quiet features, conservative movement, high cheek bones.. He did not speak English at all and the only way of communication was through another Sri Lankan prisoner who spoke some English. He told me he was waiting to be deported.

The third was from Zambia and his name was Mr. Coni. He was tall man in his mid-forties, and his hair was in the early stages of turning gray. In his eyes, I could see very deep sadness. He had a painful smile. If he laughed, it was full of bitterness. He always looked down toward the ground as if he was deeply thinking about something. He stared around him, keeping his silence. He spoke slowly and if he raised his head while speaking, he immediately put it back down. He used his hands trying to express his anger. In the middle of his speech he became silent, relaxed his hand, put his head back down, and returned to the silence. I felt as if he believed there was no point in talking. He had spent about six years in the prison as a result of being accused for a murder. He told me he was truly innocent and was praying to God to declare his innocence. He was a contractor with a company and house. He was married with a son. He was a Christian but he wanted to join our church since he followed no denomination.

I experienced the euphoria of the victorious. Three conversions in one day and not too long after starting in this service, this euphoria quickly diminished, however. It its place came a feeling of responsibility. I felt responsible for teaching them everything about Christianity and the Bible. I kept thinking of the rest of the prisoners and how much more work and guidance toward Christ they needed as well.

I asked them to wait until I finished with the other prisoners' needs. I later sat with them separately and began to explain to them about atonement – the forgiveness by blood. I told them about Jesus and how he carried our sins, and that all our sins were forgiven.

All this was completely new to them. However, the communication was not easy, with the exception of Mr. Coni. But they understood all that I told them. I organized a meeting for them after the general prison service. I was sitting with them for about an hour every time. Sometimes I went especially for them during the week to talk to them. I gave them the New Testament and I asked Mr. Coni to help them to know Jesus' miracles and life. Every time I met with them, I felt as though they were enlightened. They began telling me their stories about Jesus. One day I decided to take the next step with them.

There is no entertainment in prison. There are no sports, nor is there a gym. At most, some individual people jog and do some stationary exercises. I suggested to the prisoners to do a soccer tournament. The prison committee talked with the authorities about the idea, and they agreed. But, they asked where I would get the ball. I told them I would bring a few. I went the following Thursday and I found everyone was enthusiastic about the idea. They chose to make each cell a team. The committee organized who would play with who. They turned the arena into a field and created a watching area around the outside boundaries. I brought them a ball and it was planned that there would be two games every day. The whole tournament would finish in ten days. Their happiness and enthusiasm was palpable while they played. I was ecstatic. I never imagined that such a simple act could have this impact on them. On the day of prize distributions, I brought stuff they needed and had asked for before. Their happiness as well as mine was indescribable that day.

One day during the week, I went to sit with the three new believers to read with them the Bible. I found the one with Cameroon seemed melancholy. I took him aside and asked what troubled him. He was hesitant to tell me and even refused to look at me. When I pressed him about it, He looked down and spoke while holding back the tears. He told me he had a big problem and did not know what to do. I told him there was no problem without a solution and that he should tell me and that I could help. He began to speak with a lot of shame in his face. He had become a victim of prison rape, with the prisoners repeating and alternating among themselves. He did not know what to do. He had no money to pay for someone to protect him. I kept silent for a long time and I did not know what to answer him because I knew the depth of the problem, as I knew the prison authority would do nothing. The other prisoners could not do anything either since no one wanted to face those evil people. After a long period of silence, I asked him, "You believe in Jesus, don't you?" He answered positively. I told him, let us pray about this issue and I am sure God will intervene and save you. We prayed together and I promised him I would continue praying for this issue.

There are many events that happen to us to change the course of our lives. What happened to these three men is something that will affect the rest of their lives.

The next step I wanted to take with them was their baptism. I explained to them what it means to be "born again" and the importance of being baptized. I pointed out all Bible verses of baptism and chrismation and explained to them the baptism with immersion, three times in the water, in the name of Jesus. After that, they would participate in the communion. That session was the most wonderful session I spent with them they were very enthusiastic about the idea. However, the one from Sri Lanka was going to be deported at any time. So they asked to be baptized and receive the Eucharist as soon as possible. I spoke to the father and prison authorities and we choose a day for the baptism. . I asked them to prepare a barrel to clean and use in their baptism. We went about an hour earlier than our appointed time to ensure that everything was well prepared. I was surprised because many of the prisoners helped them to prepare for their baptism and others gave them new clothes to wear after baptism, while others gave them towels. Their baptism was an indescribable moment for me and I will never forget it.

After one week, I visited them and found a large number of prisoners wanting to be baptized. I found the three men completely different and told them they really felt as if they were born again. The one from Sri Lanka was about to leave in a few days. He told me that he would tell his family about all that had happened and about Christianity so that they may believe in Him. The one from Cameroon, told me he is eager to know more about our church. Mr. Coni told me that when he gets released, he will work with me as a missionary.

A week later, the one from Sri Lanka was deported to his country and the signs of illness began to appear on the one from Cameroon. He told me God answered the prayers and no one would rape him anymore. His illness began to worsen hastily until he was unable to walk. They began to carry him from the cell on a stretcher to the meeting place in the arena. In vain they tried to treat him as if he had pneumonia. But I knew that he was infected by HIV.

One day I visited him and I knew this was going to be the last time I was going to see him. His face was very pale, but an unusual peace covered his face with a calm smile. He told me that he was going to leave this place and go back to his home looking up to heaven. He continued, only now I know why I came to this place . To know you and become a Christian. He began coughing badly and he continued, "You are the only one that gave me love in this place." I began to console him. I asked him when he would go back to his home to pray for me.

I had to leave Zambia for a while. When I returned, I had heard he left to his heavenly home as a stranger, in a strange land. I was not there to take care of his final needs. I knew that he was buried in the pottery field in Lusaka.

A majority of the prisoners, when they get out of prison, visit us in the mission station. Some of them ask for money so they can return to their homes, others come for friendship and to join the church. One day I was surprised by Mr. Coni standing in front of me smiling. He told me he was set free because they found him innocent after he had spent six years in prison. His wife divorced him while he was in prison and married his friend. She took his house and his car and she is very sick, near death. He has to look out for his son, who is jobless and homeless. He also lost his company, too. He told me he wants to start a new life regardless of all that he lost. He has two freedoms now, his freedom from the prison and his freedom from sin when he became a Christian. "I have been transferred from dark to light and you help me with that," Mr. Coni continued.

Mr. Coni joined our theological school and became an active member in our ministry and began working in the mission hospital maintenance. He found his fifteen-year-old son and lived with him. He also began to get to know a woman from our church and they are preparing to get engaged as I'm writing this now.

Before I left Zambia, I notice Mr. Coni was not speaking to me. He intentionally avoided me. He also avoided eye contact with me and it had me wondering the reason. When I asked him, he looked at me and left without an answer. A few days before I left, he came to my house during the evening and asked me, "Is it true you are leaving Zambia and leaving me?" I told him that God was calling me to serve Him in another place. I told him I would always be in contact with him. He put his head down as he always did and the tears started running from his eyes. He asked me with whom am I going to leave him with. He told me he would be an orphan after I left. I was touched by his words. I felt I was unworthy for all this love. He asked me in pain, "Is there any way I can get you to stay?" I answered him, "I will always be with you in your prayers." He told me that he was born in my hands and that I had helped him to be transformed from darkness into the light, and that I was with him during the times of tribulation. Then he looked at me and said, "I will never forget you in all my life." He hugged me and we began crying.

These were honest feelings. They expressed their feelings honestly because this was all they had. They accepted any simple thing as it came directly from God's hand. You saw love and gratitude in their eyes. It is easy for them to know who really loves them. Our ministry to them is nothing. Jesus is the only one that can make things new.

Concluded
Guinea, Conakry
April, 2007

Kevin

Have you ever experienced being crushed completely, completely at a loss for hope? To the point where you could not fathom a glimmer of change? If you have ever experienced this, you will understand Kevin's story.

Kevin is a man of twenty years of age. He is from one of the north district villages in Zambia. His father deceased a while ago. He is the third of four brothers. It was a miracle that he finished his basic education, as the rest of his siblings had not finished with some still attending school and has no hope of finishing.

His mother spares no effort in providing their daily bread. Her sons try to help her. Every morning, they go to the forest to collect as much mango and mushrooms as they can. When money gets tight, they go to nearby cities to work menial jobs. The wages they received is not enough for their basic needs. Their only hope was for Kevin was to become a teacher. But how would he be able to finish his education? How would he be able to pay the university fees? It is nearly impossible to get a scholarship.

I entered the mission station and drove my car to the parking lot. I walked through the walkway in the mission garden, which was beautiful and carefully trimmed. There were flowers on both sides of the walkway, and the trees distributed in a perfect landscape. It was considered a wonderful place for meditation and quiet time in the midst of the mission station. On the north side, there is a straw sunshade where we sometimes held meetings.

I went to my house and saw a man sitting under the sunshade. The night was progressing. I was surprised by someone sitting under the sunshade this late in the day. I went to him and greeted him good evening. I asked if there was anything I could help him with.

"No thank you I am just sitting," He answered. I told him, "It is quite late and this area is for the missionary housing."

"Really? I did not know. It seems I have to go." He answered sheepishly.

I felt that I had embarrassed him.. Many thieves would come during the day to spy on the place in order to know who was living there and where so that they could attack or hijack at another time. Because of that, we were not allowed to let any person sit or walk nearby the missionaries' housing

"I am sorry, I did not mean to chase you away, but I wanted to help you if you needed anything."

"Well I was just sitting." He continued, "Do you know me?"

I looked at him carefully in hopes of remembering him. His face was not the type that was easily forgotten. He was tall, with heavy naturally-spiked hair and on his forehead above his right eye was a five centimeter diameter bony protrusion which made his eye squint. Oblate lips, snubbed nose, with strong features. You saw both determination and sadness in his eyes. He had a nice smile that, to me, reflected a good-heart. But after a while of trying to remember, I answered him, "I'm sorry, I do not remember you."

"I have recently been coming to the youth meeting every Sunday."

"Do you enjoy it?"

"Yes, very much he answered," nodding his head.

"Where do you live, and what are you doing here in Lusaka?"

"I am from the North district and I now live with some of my friends looking for a job and finishing my education here in Lusaka." We left the sunshade and walked toward the main gate. I shacked his hand saying, "My name is Isaac, you may ask about me if you need anything and they will tell you where I am."

"My name is Kevin. Nice meeting you Mr. Isaac."

The next time I saw him was at the Sunday service and after that at the youth meeting. I saw him repeatedly sit under the sunshade alone, especially at sunset. Usually he looked as if he was thinking about something. But he never asked for helped or wanted to talk, as most people did.

One morning, I found Kevin sitting under the sunshade. I went to him and greeted him. Briefly he replied to my greetings as it seemed he did not want to be disturbed. He appeared sad and weary but it was not physical weariness, it was more like emotional exhaustion. I sat beside him and asked him what was wrong. He turned his head to me, then returned staring off in the distance and answered, "I have a problem and I do not know what to do."

I looked at him encouraging him to speak and he continued "My roommate asked me to pay my portion of the rent but I do not have money." I knew from him that he stayed with one of his friends and he slept on the bare floor without a pillow. His friend had torn blankets that he covered himself with as he slept. He paid his friend 25,000 kwacha which is about five dollars monthly. I asked him, "What about your basic needs like food and clothing?"

He replied with a question, "Where would I get these?" but he continued, "God provides."

I asked him again, "You do not work?"

He answered, "I do not have a stable job. Every day I look for a job to pay my rent and to feed myself but on many days I do not find. When I get tired at sunset, I come here and sit under the sunshade to cool down, relax think what to do and pray to God to guide me."

I found in Kevin something unusual. Something different than all the people that asked for help. The difference was that he did not ask for anything. He was just sharing with me his problem. He only did this because I asked him. If I had not requested of him, he would not have informed me. Even though Kevin did not ask for money or aid, I decided to give him the money he needed and a little more for a few days. He thanked me when I told him that but he claimed, "This is not my main problem."

I began to be doubtful of his issues because as I had experienced, when I help someone with a small amount of money, they begin to ask for more.

I asked him, "What is your main problem?"

He answered, "I want to finish my education and be a teacher." I really respected him when he said this, because he knew exactly what he wanted and did not ask for anything.

I told him, "I can help you in that too."

He looked at me carelessly as if he did not believe me and asked me how.

I told him that I would pay for his school fees to pursue teaching. He did not believe what he heard. He said "It is costly and quite expensive."

I had no idea about the cost of his study which he wanted to finish. I had not known what I promised him was right or wrong. I was hasty in my decision especially since he was new to the church and no one knew him well enough. There are some people that join the church to receive benefits then leave. I asked him to go and ask about the cost of his education and the method of payment, then come and tell me. I gave him the money he needed for the rent and basic needs for a couple of days.

Next day in the afternoon, he came to my house and thanked me for my help. He said that there is a two-year institution that gives educational diplomas from Britain and they evaluated my degree and gave me acceptance to enroll with them. I found enthusiasm in his eyes and asked him how much would the cost be for the first year. He answered about 300 sterling without the book and exam fees. We can pay monthly, but we have to pay the first the months as a first installment. I felt the cost was too much for me. It means I have to pay first installment about $120 and $40 every month plus the book and exam fees. I was thinking if I had implicated myself in this situation. From where could I get this money every month? Even if I had some money, there were many expenses in the service and ministry. But I felt as if Kevin was drowning and I threw to him a lifeline. So I decided to help him with whatever the cost was. I looked to his eyes and told him, "I will pay it for you." I found on his face a smile of gratitude. He did not believe that his dream would finally come true. Before the time of enrollment closed we paid the first three months. Usually, I do not give the money to the one I am helping with directly. Many take the money and spend it on urgent needs. I usually send a servant to pay the fees and return a receipt to me. But with Kevin, it was a different situation.

We only help those who were serious about their education and I found that seriousness in Kevin. After he started, I began to see him only on Sundays and on Wednesday evenings. I would always see him carrying books. During the weekends, he came and studied under the sunshade. Kevin had a very clear target and insisted on reaching it. We solved the problem of his education but what about the issue of his basic needs? Kevin did chores around the mission station and was compensated so that he could pay for his needs. He was studying in every possible place, in the mission station, parks, sometimes even in the malls. Anywhere he was able to study. Kevin was not able to buy all the books for that, he paid to borrowing books from the library. One day he came to my house and it seemed he needed something but was unable to talk. Instead he just said he came to see me because we had not met for a while. Two days later, I met him inside the mission station. It appeared as if he wanted to say something but he did not tell me even after asking. Later one evening, I saw him under the sunshade without any books but returned to his thinking. I came closer and after I greeted him I asked him if there is anything he wants to tell me or talk about. He said it direct, "I can't borrow any books from the library because I lost my biology book. I have to pay insurance to borrow another book." Insurance is about $8 of their currency and he needs to study especially because the midterm exam is very soon. He is too shy to ask for more because he already asked for many things and he does not want me to think that he is using me. I looked at his eyes and said, "I know you aren't using me. The most important thing is for you to finish your studies and become a teacher."

The exam fee was the big obstacle. It was about $160 sterling. An amount I was unable to pay, so I borrowed it. I have seen Kevin studying very hard. He wasted nothing of his time. He never drank or went out with women. He wanted to see the fruit of his works and getting this diploma was the first step of his dream.

On the day the school released the results, his joy and happiness were indescribable. However, there was no one to share with him his success, except me. Both of us felt the sense of success. I personally felt his success. Kevin finished both years with high grades and got his diploma. He started to look for a job. I thought it would be easy for him to find a job as a teacher with his certificate but I was wrong. Although the government is in desperate need for teachers, there are no schools to accommodate them. The private schools, although there are many of them, are staffed and prefer individuals with bachelor degrees. I was confused about the situation. Kevin began being depressed because after all this hard work, investment, deprivation, and toiled in studying he cannot work as a teacher. He had to go back to the low and menial jobs he worked before.

After a few months Kevin disappeared, I also left Zambia. When I came back, I asked about him but no one knew his whereabouts as he never came in the last few months. I thought he got what he needed and would never return. After a while, I found him sitting under the sunshade as usual. I went to greet him and when he saw me he came towards me to greet me too. He said, "I went to your house and I did not find you."

I asked him, "Where have you been all this time?"

He said he went back to his mother and stayed with her all this time. He looked for teaching jobs but in vain. I asked him what he was planning to do. He said, "I am trying to finish my bachelor degree so that I can work as a teacher with a decent salary."

I was looking at him wondering how he was doing without resources, help, or any consolidation. He continued persevering to reach his target. Many people become depressed and Kevin was very poor, slept on the floor, covered himself with torn blankets, slept with no pillow, and many times slept without supper. There was not even any light in his house. Despite all of those obstacles, he was still focused on his destination. I wish those who have the resources, and an easy life, yet still complain, try to understand where Kevin is coming from and what he is accomplishing without complaint. In Africa there are many intelligent students who do not receive an education because they are unable to pay for their school fees. I wonder about this paradox of a young man who has nothing but the determination and those who have resources that are wasted in unmotivated individuals. What would Kevin's situation be if he was only given half the resources that are available to those in developed countries? I had no doubt that even with his circumstances, he would reach his goals.

Kevin told me that he would apply for a scholarship as his solution. I know there are many scholarships available for advanced students, but because of corruption, the scholarships do not make it to the worthy. Kevin had no real chance of getting one.

I offered him luck and then he proceeded to tell me there was something he needed from me.

"What is it?" I asked

"Pray for me to get a scholarship."

I promised I would do so. He returned to his usual routine in the prayer meeting and we began to spend more time together. He returned to the menial jobs he dreaded in order to meet his basic needs.

Before I left Zambia for my annual vacation, the youth had thrown a little goodbye party. Kevin was there. After the party concluded, Kevin asked me to take a walk with him. While we were walking, he turned with happiness on his face and said, "You were my father and my brother during this time. Without you, I could have not accomplished anything."

"You are wrong. You are the one that studied, suffered, and passed through all the obstacles." He told me he filled out the application for a scholarship and was waiting for the decision. I encouraged him saying, "I'm sure you will get one."

"I wish that from all my heart," Kevin replied.

When I returned from my vacation, I found Kevin waiting for me at the main gate of the mission station. After putting my luggage down, he told me that he was offered a scholarship. He would be receiving his bachelor's degree after three more years of college. The schooling he had already done saved him one year.

I hugged him joyfully and he continued, "They will give me pocket money every month and I promised I will help a child who is unable to pay for their school fees. After I finish my bachelor's degree, I will pursue my masters."

I was proud of him and his diligence. I wanted to tell many about his story. Kevin is one of many good students who struggle to complete their education.

Kevin was the first spark for a program we began in the mission for those who are serious in finishing their education as this is their golden opportunity to get a real job with a good income. The goal of the School Fees program is to help serious students finish their education and they, in return help more students finish theirs. With this program, we have helped 50 students in different grades. Six of them finished their bachelor's degree. We have also successfully launched this program in Kenya. As it says in China, "Give a fish you will feed me for a meal. Teach me how to fish and you will feed me for a lifetime."

Repentance Story

Sin is the heaviest yoke a man can carry. Guilt is the hardest feeling to endure. Humans are burdened with the plague of sin. Man tries to get rid of the consequence and punishment of sin, but to no avail Enter Christ, who offers in this instance, the meaning of autonomy, that we place the burden of sin upon Jesus on the cross. I asked the individual to whom I presented this message of salvation, "What are you doing to receive forgiveness for your sins?" After a period of silence, he began telling me about traditions, offerings and other things he must do in order to receive forgiveness. I asked him, "After you do all these things, do you truly feel forgiveness in your heart and assurance you will be with Him in heaven?".

I have not found a single person from any religion that was assured that he would be forgiven and given salvation, with the exception of Christianity.

In Christianity it's different. Christianity has offered for us the principle of free salvation. More accurately, we receive it freely when we accept Jesus as our personal savior who has already paid the price of sin, by His blood, on the cross. This is the greatness of Christianity. It gives us the core solution for the problem of sin. Imagine a person who is in deep debt and is unable to pay. He goes to meet the bank manager and is told, "We can facilitate for you easily payable installments." Is this person no longer responsible for his debt? Of course not, he still must pay it. Now this is the good news. Imagine the same person with the same debt going to the bank manager and informing him, "Your debt has completely been erased, someone has paid it. He deposited a million dollars into your account. This is exactly what Jesus did. He paid the debt for our sin and deposited into our account an eternal glory to withdraw from while we are on earth.

The Lord Jesus gave an appeal to everyone that feels the burden of sin. What truly sad is that there are many Christians who still live under this heavy burden of sin and the illusion of its authority upon them. They have not learned to put their sin on the cross and confess in order to receive forgiveness and peace. "He who covers his sins will not prosper, But whoever confesses and forsakes them will have mercy". (Proverbs 28:13)

I was in a youth convention in Johannesburg, South Africa. All the youth had come from different churches to attend the convention. I enjoy a mixture of youth especially at conventions in order to help them with their problems and needs. One evening during the convention, we were watching the life of St. Marina. I was translating explaining, and giving a commentary on the film. The hall contained more than one hundred youth. The lights were off and I was informing them about St. Marina and how she conquered Satan, refused sin, and withstood lust. While I explained this to them, the room was silent. I could only see their white eyes and teeth. I saw a young lady I knew because we had chatted for a little while together. She wept in silence and no one noticed her tears but me. After the movie, I asked her why she was crying. She answered, "I wish one day to be like St. Marina."

"How does this relate to your crying? You can be like her." I asked.

"It's very hard. Extremely hard," she replied.

"Why?"

"There are many sins and foolish deeds I have done in my life that I cannot get rid of."

"Are you serious in your repentance and to leave the way of sin?" She told me she left the way of sin a while ago but does not feel forgiven. There is a bitter feeling of guilt. "The solution is very simple. Repent and confess and this feeling will go away."

She answered with tears in her eyes, "I can't. I can't confess."

"You will never feel peace until you confess. Confess and offer sincere repentance to God and you will find rest."

She did not answer. We had to hurry to the church with the rest of the group to begin the prayer meeting. During the prayers I poured myself to God for her sake. I asked Him to give her the power to confess to Him all her sins. After almost thirty minutes of prayer, I saw her going to the altar area. I knew my prayers had been answered.

Next day, I saw her with a joyful face. She came to me happily saying, "How awesome is the sacrament of confession." She continued, "This is the greatness of our God. All I have to do is just to put my sin under His cross and confess".

Truly as St. John said, "If we confess with our sins he is honest and the blood of Jesus purifies us from all our sins." (1 John 1:19).

A Tale of a Church 1

Behind the establishment of every church, there is a story. Most of them are stories of faith that declare God's wonderful work. The evil one can't accept, but cannot tolerate the existence of God's house to gather the believers and pray. He then desperately attempts to sabotage the building of any church. This is what I have seen and experienced in not only Egypt,_but in the mission too. Many countries allow and support the building of churches but the evil one does not want that. However in some countries the evil one uses the government and non-believers to halt the establishment of a church. It is the same in the mission field.

In missionary work, we normally do not build a church until we "build" the people. We build the hearts before we build the bricks. What's the purpose of a building without believers? Therefore we evangelize the people first. After they accept Jesus and get baptized, they build a church for themselves, and we help them with it. This is exactly what happened in the Mongoli.

The Mongoli is a bush area about forty five miles northwest of the capital Lusaka in Zambia. With a population of about eighteen thousand a majority of which were illiterate. In August 2001, we started the ministry there. We were going once a week and divided ourselves into small groups of two or three. The missionaries with the local servants and each group would go to one or two villages to evangelize. Once a month we would go to spend with them three to five days. This area in the middle of the forest appealed to me because it was very far from civilization. No electricity, running water, internet, phones, or even homes to live in. We were sleeping in tents with no restrooms. It is the very image of the first primitive life of man. There, the night is extravagant. You see the sky full of stars and you feel it is very close. I was feeling great peace during my sleep. Fear never penetrated me. However, many people warned me of snakes and scorpions I would never get hurt. I would sleep like a baby guarded by his mother.

I remember the first time I visited Zambia. One of the church members from England joined our church after he studied our doctrine and loved it. He took me in his Jeep on my last day in Zambia to Mongoli. He told me, "All these souls are desperate and thirsty for God's word." This trip was the main reason; I went back to Zambia to consecrate my time to evangelism, especially for the bush areas. I felt in this visit God was calling me for the ministry in this place.

The people over there are not just poor, but are destitute. Every year, they pass through true famine for three months every year. Starting from December through March. This is because last year's crops are finished and they are in the waiting period for the new crops.

After one year of evangelism in many villages, about one hundred and seventy people had believed. After another year the number had reached almost two hundred and fifty. In 2005, we had baptized over 400 people. God is still joining new people every day.

After some time evangelizing, a wealthy man named Mr. Mayoni and his family joined the church and donated 20 acres to the church. When we started to register this land under the church name, I had to travel to another governor to finish all the paperwork, the bureaucracy took way too much time and effort.

One day, I met the committee and they saw all the paperwork, designs, drawings, and what we were going to do with the land. They were very cooperative, which I was not expecting. They gave us a temporary title deed until we could get the original one from the land ministry.

While we were going back to the mission station, I was thinking at how everything was going perfectly and unexpectedly fast. I was worried that the devil was going to envy our progress and start to intervene, especially since there was another piece of land in the capital Lusaka where we had finished the paperwork and had already begun building the church. As soon as I finished thinking about that, the driver hit a young man riding his bicycle. The young man suddenly crossed the highway horizontally. Upon impact the young man flew through the windshield and landed right on me and was reflected back to the road side motionless. All this happened in the blink of an eye. The driver stopped. The front part of the car was completely destroyed. The radiator of the car was damaged and was not holding any water. Many people from the village on the road side came to see what had happened. I bought from them a drum of water to fill the radiator constantly and we went to the nearest checkpoint which was about a mile away. The car was not moving more than twenty kilometers per hour. We had to stop often to fill the radiator. At the checkpoint, two officers came back with us to the young man corpse and put it, with his bicycle in the back of the pickup truck. We went to the nearest police station to finish the procedures.

Two months after this horrible accident, while we were building a church in Lusaka for one of our new congregation, we were fixing the ceiling The carpenter ran out of nails. I asked the driver (a new driver) to go and buy nails from the nearest hardware store before it closes so we could finish the ceiling.

I warned the new driver to be careful, so as to avoid giving any chance to the evil one to disturb our work. On our way back, the driver was trying to cut off the car in front of him. Suddenly the driver of this car tried to cut off the car in front of him. We were almost beside him; he had not checked us in his side mirror. As the vehicle approached us, our driver diverted to the right to avoid collision. As a result he hit a woman carrying an infant on her back. I asked the driver to go back quickly and I found the child had died and the woman's leg was broken. We carried the infant and woman in the back of our truck. We drove to the nearest community hospital. On our way, I was dropped off to go to the missions station to tell the father and the doctor in charge of the mission clinic to come with me to help bring this woman to the mission clinic and to finish the procedures faster. When the three of us had arrived, the police officer had told us that the driver had given her the car keys and told her that he had hit this woman and her child and that this car belongs to the Coptic mission and that we were coming. Then he escaped. The officer told us this was typical, that drivers hit someone and escape for fear of punishment, but come back after few days.

Three days passed and the driver had not come. One week passed and the driver had still not come. To close the police report and in order for the woman to receive her compensation, the woman was told to accuse me of driving the vehicle, for I was a foreigner. And though the police knew I was not the driver, they started following me to arrest me.

The building of the church was delayed. I understood and realized the war that the evil on wages on completing the church. The first car was destroyed in the first accident. The second one was confined within the police station and the police were looking for me.

The built church was six miles away from the mission station in Northmead , Lusaka. After we finished all the paperwork and went with the bishop to start the work. Suddenly a large crowd of people surrounded us carrying swords, knives, and bats and prevented us from starting work. A crook had sold small pieces of the church land (about seven acres) to individuals for a cheap price. The people told us to leave the land or they will kill us and bury us on our land. The bishop asked us to leave peacefully without a problem. After many calls and meetings with the authorities, the land was returned to us, without paying any money.

On that particular day one of the crook's helpers told me, "You will never build a church in this place." I later found out he was a devil worshiper. I told him, "You will see a house of God in this place." A few months later, after we finished the church, I met him. We chatted for a while. He told me, truly what happened was more than a miracle. Many of the devil worshipers tried black magic to prevent the work but it had no effect. He decided to leave devil worshiping and to follow the church. I told him, "Even if there is black magic, it has no authority over God's sons.

After the second accident, the ceiling's wood needed to be transported from the storage to the building site. The distance was only about two hundred feet, but the wood was big and heavy. Nevertheless, we carried the wood from the storage to the building site on our shoulders. I said to the devil, "Do what you like but we will continue working.".

During these trials, my trust toward God multiplied. But after the second accident, I asked God to remove this tribulation from me and to allow us to continue the work.

After we finished the ceiling frame and were waiting to fix the ceiling the next day, I went home. An hour later, someone knocked on my door. When I opened, I found the side guard telling me that the ceiling frame had fallen down as a result of very strong wind but that, thankfully, no one got hurt. It was very clear what the evil one was attempting to do. Whatever prayers and intercessions we asked for, we thought, maybe that was not enough. Very deep peace was inside me. The priest and I went to the work site and what we saw hurt us deeply. We built many ceilings and nothing like this had happened before. But when you build a church, it's completely different.

We successfully finished building the St. Mary church six miles away from the mission station on the very land that they threatened us from starting the work.

Now beside the church, there is a convention building that can accommodate up to fifty persons, a school, a clinic and a big house for the missionaries.

All of this exemplifies God's great glory and support. Truly without him we can do nothing.

Now let us go back to Mongolia:

After the number of believes increased, it became of the utmost importance to have a church for them. Seasonally, they were building a church from mud and straw. But during the rainy season, the church would demolish. This would happen every year. They told me they are willing to work to finish their own church.

There were many obstacles. The place was very far from the city, and to buy the building material and send it there would very expensive. Moreover, it is very difficult to live in the bush area. As there is no accommodation for the long period of work, effort, and organization.

I presented all these obstacles to the believers. They were willing to endure all these difficulties. I suggested that instead of transporting all the materials from the city, that we prepare the materials ourselves. A group of people would go to the edge of the forest to collect big rocks to be crushed to stones. Another group goes to a water stream four miles away to bring sand for building. I brought for them the cement and the model to model the bricks. It takes to prepare all the building materials and all the bricks about one year and a half. After we finished preparing all the materials we started digging the foundation. On the working site, there was no nearby water. The nearest well was about two miles away. The women divided themselves into four groups. Each group about four or five women. Three groups are responsible for drawing water, each group working for three hours. Each woman after that returns to her home to her duties. The fourth group was responsible for preparing the food for the workers. The work was an story of love. The new believers have nothing to offer but themselves. They worked with enthusiasm and love.

Many of the events that transpired showed me the nature of these people and the amount of their love. Before we could begin digging the foundation, we needed to remove all of the bushes, roots, and clean the area. While we were doing this, I found a man next to me digging frantically and excitingly. When I asked why this was, he told me he had found dinner for his family tonight. He held out to me some roots from the bushes, and told me that they boil it and eat it. I explained to him it looks like potatoes but it has lots of fiber.

There was another man, Fine who was sick during the period we began building. Although he was sick and lived over seven miles away, he would bring milk to the workers each day because he had cows. He claimed that this was his contribution. Even though he could not work, he did not want to miss out on the blessings.

Another man, Kalema worked hard for twelve hours straight the entire time we were building I had not been paying wages for the workers, I was just offering meals. In return they had not asked for money, they felt as if they were building their own church and it was their responsibility. They needed support, not wages.

All the work was complete in almost six months. It was a truly joyful day when the work had been completed and we began praying in our new church.

My beloved, there are many stories about the building and planting of church. This is only one of many that explains the relentless war the devil wages to prevent the establishment of a church. But, at the same time, it declares God's wonder, support, and I do not_mistake any establishment of a church is a miracle in itself. I encourage you to write and tell others if you pass through a similar experience so that we may know God's work in the church. I ask of you to pray for the people of Lynga tribe in the Mongoli area and for all other unreachable villages till now.

Simple Faith

After we had completed the church building and the church was ready to be prayed in, we were able to begin praying and holding meetings. We could not contain our happiness. However, we could not enjoy this happiness for too long, because soon after, the people sent me a letter asking me to come because a very strong wind had removed part of the roof. The rains were heavy and were flooding into the church through the damaged roof. I was crushed. I asked all the believers to assemble for a prayer meeting and to intercede to revoke Satan's work. I began to tell them about the devil's war against the church and how he can endure the presence of a church. During my sermon, there was a man sitting on a brick because the pews were not yet in place. This man moved unusually, jumped quickly, and lifted up the brick only to find a large poisonous snake under the brick. Very quickly and skillfully he threw the brick on the snake's head and killed it. Here we had become sure that the evil one was playing a role in these events. All of us stood to pray and their prayers were full of fervor for the sake of protecting their church.

A few days later, I went back to the church congregation to pray with them about evangelizing the other villages. While we were praying, I heard moaning as if someone was trying to cry. Soon it turned into screaming. When I looked, I found a woman that I later found out was an unbeliever. She was wallowing on the ground and screaming indiscernible words. I recognized she was demon-possessed. It was my first time to experience such a person. The new believers of the church quickly made a circle around her and began singing and praying quietly, but with importunity to the Lord to cast out her unclean spirit. This they had learned from my telling them about Jesus' many miracles where He cast out demons and rebuked unclean spirits. They did this spontaneously, without being asked to do so. In that moment, I learned from their simple faith. They prayed until the unclean spirit left her and she stood upright normally and we finished the prayer meeting joyfully.

Later on, Zambia passed through famine, because the rainy season had come late that year, so they began planting the seeds late. The rainy season ended at the beginning of February, which meant that the corn harvest would die, causing true famine. The rainy season was supposed to continue up till the end of April. This occurred in 2003. All of Zambia was praying for this matter.

The Mongolie church congregation sent a letter to the mission station so that I may go to them and pray to God to send rain and save their crops that year. On the day we had designated for prayer, I was on my way to them and there was not a single cloud in the sky. The sun was out; the weather was dry, humidity high, and no signs of rain. I said to myself that we would pray today and maybe God will send rain tomorrow, or in the near future. When I had arrived to the church I had found the congregation had already assembled and started prayer. They were praying and singing passionately and when I looked to them they were completely mesmerized in prayer. The prayer meeting continued for about three hours. After we finished, I was supposed to return before sunset because of the long distance. When we walked out of the church I found the sky, which was previously cloudless, became black with very heavy clouds. The sun which was previously out was nowhere to be seen. There were warning signs for the coming of very heavy rains. The people asked me to leave as soon as possible so that the rain would not prevent me from driving, as there are many areas in the bushes that are rugged and impossible to drive through with heavy rain, even if you have a 4x4 vehicle.

When I began driving, the rains began. Within a few minutes, it was pouring. I saw people jogging joyfully, not only for the rain but because Christ had answered their prayers. What was really amazing was five miles away from this village, there was no rain and the sun was out. I understood and knew that God had answered the prayers of the new believers for their simple faith. All these events were to strengthen my weak faith and reproach me as I had not reached their simple faith.

Church Tale 2

Our God is the God of the impossible. There is nothing He cannot do or change, even if it seems impossible. He is capable of changing laws, systems, and governors. The more difficult the situation, the more God's work will become clear. God's work starts, when man stops. When man surrenders and he is unable to take any further action, this is when God begins to work..

This story begins in Eligo a village in Maseno, Kenya. This church was built there after our service started in this area and believers were baptized. The available land for the church was close to a railway. The church construction was finished in record time. Everyone helped and the congregation's joy was palpable for their church. But how can the evil one allow this? It was very difficult for him to see a new church born in this area which was previously under his control. The church was helping the whole area, and not the church members only.

For whatever reason, a decision came from city hall to demolish all the buildings within three hundred meters of the railroad. This meant the church would be demolished. The father in charge went to visit the authorities trying to convince them to exclude the church from this decision. For what the church offers for all the people in the area, but his efforts fell in vain.

The congregation was confused. They were unable to do anything. They tried to complain and appeal but nothing worked. They placed their appeals on the owner of the church. They decided to pray and fast inside the church for three days, asking God to cancel this decision and protect their church, for which they waited for a long time. They assembled the prayer meeting, and other churches came to share in prayer with them. After the third day, everyone went to His home with faith that God will do something for his church and this was the case. Another decision was put in place to decrease the distance from three hundred meters to only two hundred meters.. The church was now safe from being demolished. This is how God saved his church with the prayer of the people. Truly our God is the God of the impossible.

Part 2
Service in Egypt

Richer than Everyone

Do you know what poverty means? Maybe you've heard about it. Most probably you have not bothered yourself to know its nature and dimensions. If you have a desire for something and have the money to purchase it, that means you are not poor. For example, if you would like to eat something special and you are capable of paying for it, you are not poor. When your desire exceeds your purchase ability you feel like you are poor. For example, you want to buy a luxury car. You don't have the money to buy the luxury car, now you feel poor. But, if you desire nothing but food and clothes to cover your body, you are richer than everyone. Not because you have a lot of money, but because you desire nothing.

But this is not the poverty I mean. But by the end of this story, you will know what true poverty is.

The reason I enjoy writing so much is that I am in control of everything. I can make someone live, and another die. Make someone rich and another one poor. I can conclude my story however I want. You, my beloved reader's role is completely passive. You can only react to the drama I am writing, but you can't interfere with the story. But my role becomes very limited if I am writing the truth. I become controlled by the reality of the story. A reality I must follow. The most I can do is adapt the language to describe events. However, your role has not changed. You are still the recipient for the events and you have no control. Because of this, I would like to change your role which you will know after this story.

Teresa, is about to finish her fifties but the first time you see her, she looks over eighty. We can't call her slim. Teresa is a group of bones assembled together covered with a thin layer of skin, to form a human. Her hunchback makes her appear shorter than she really is. She has no eyes but two holes in her face because she is blind. She lives in the ruins of her house. One day it was a house built from mud, but the next it was demolished. The only part that remained was a small entrance. Some good people repaired the entrance by placing a woven ceiling above her, so that she may sleep. The rest of the house was left in ruin in which she passed bowels, because she has no restroom. A small black curtain differentiated between her entrance and her ruins.

Teresa has no one to take care of her. Her husband passed away and her daughter is mentally deranged, married to a handicapped man. Her daughter does not have enough food to take care of her family, so there is no way they would be able to take care of Teresa. Teresa lives alone in this cave, I call it a cave because she has no light during the evening.

We met Teresa and she joined our ministry. Our ministry was called "Those who Have No One to Remember Them." Some servants from the ministry made her cave habitable. They fixed a door, and they created a defined separation between the entrance and her ruins. All these improvements she paid no attention to. She was very thankful when we gave her a mat and pillow to sleep on. This also was not something of large impact to her. Although Teresa was poverty-stricken, she never complained any day, not once. Every time we asked her if she needed anything, she would thank us saying she did not. We discovered that most days, she did not have her basic food necessities nor did she ask for them.

One day we asked her if she had something for supper. She said there were a few rice grains she would eat. When we looked for the rice, we found an empty pot. So we asked her again where the rice was, and she said it was in the pot. There were two spoons of rice in the pot.. Literally, there were no more than two spoons of rice in the pot. We brought her something for supper. When we visited her the next day we were surprised she did not eat. When we asked her why she did not eat what we brought her for supper, she said she had eaten the two spoons of rice and that was enough.

One day after Easter, we went to visit Teresa, she told us a funny story about her. She had a neighbor from time to time that gave her food. Yesterday she gave her roasted chicken but she was not hungry at that time. So she placed it aside until she would feel hungry. What she did not know is that there was a cat who had her eye on the chicken and in the blink of an eye, the cat ate it. No one discovered what the cat did until a neighbor saw, while the cat was finishing it. Teresa was saying in simplicity,, "The cat thought the roasted chicken was too much for me to eat."

Teresa never knew what her next meal would be or where it would come from. When we asked, her answer was always, "God will provide." All that she knew was that God would never forsake her and He will provide for her needs. She always ate thankfully and always sang. Every time we visited her, we would find her singing. She was memorizing hundreds of songs and that was the only entertainment in her loneliness.

Once a month, we would take all those whom we were serving, like Teresa, and have a meeting with them starting with the morning mass followed by a meal and after that we would have fun activities. This monthly meeting was like a feast for Teresa because this was the only day she got out of her cave. Every time we went to pick her up for the meeting, she was always praying. Nothing prevented her from going, whether it was the winter cold or the summer heat. Even when she was sick. Many of the servants after visiting and talking to her would wonder about her living situation and they would feel a great peace when they were with her. She had nothing but was always very happy and her speech always radiated with joy and humor.

One day Teresa was absent from the monthly meeting. When we asked the people responsible for bringing her, they replied that she was very ill which made us very worried about her. After the liturgy, we went to her quickly to find that she passed in peace, without pain, or noise. There was no one to take her in her final moments except the servants who loved her and had been loved by her. Even at her funeral, there was no one at all because there was no one to remember her in this world.

Now my dear reader, maybe you were affected by this story. Maybe you felt some pity for her. Maybe you were not moved. My aim in telling this story was not for you to feel pity but to know your role and what you are supposed to do. Do you know what that is?

Before I answer this question, I want you to know first, what true poverty is. Poverty does not mean you have less or you can't purchase what you desire, but it means you do not know when or where your next meal is coming from. It means to sleep in the open air, homeless and if you die no one would take care of your final needs. Those, my dear reader, are not a small number. Your role is to look for them and help them. To find another Teresa and take care of her. Do not say, "From where can I know these people." You have to look for them. Many people like Teresa are waiting for you. But before you go to help them, you have to know they are not poor, but are richer than everyone.

Kitten Meat

Steve, a young man was at the end of his twenties. He worked as a teacher in the village he grew up in. He lived among his family which consisted of a father who worked as a farmer, a mother who was a housewife, three boys, and two girls. As a result of their poverty, none of them were able to finish school except Steve; he got a bachelor's degree.

Their house was similar to most of the houses in the villages in Egypt. It was built by mud with a woven ceiling. Some of the rich people would use palm trees as a roof. They did not have a restroom in their home, like most of the people in the village. But they have a small hole in one of the house corners, in which they do their bowel movements. They do not have furniture as we know, but they built a box of mud near a wall and use it as a sitting area and bed if needed. There is only one bed at home but it is not enough for the family. Each one leaves the bed for the other and sleeps on the floor or the mud box. Most of the time, the bed is Steve's share because he was the educated one in the family, and he is the only one studying at home. So his parents would prefer giving it to him instead of the rest of the family. What bothered Steve was that his mother preferred him over his siblings. He was saddened by his family's situation and felt he was responsible to take them out of this miserable life. Not only because he was the oldest, most educated, and worked a stable job, but because he was the only one that understood the depth of their poverty. He had seen the big difference between their life and the life he had seen in high school and college in the city.

It did not hurt him because he was poor, as most of the people in the villages were poor, but what hurt him most was the situation of his family. His immediate younger brother, dropped out of middle school, as most kids his age do. He went to large cities to work menial jobs and stopped asking about his family. The second youngest was working with his dad in the field and also dropped out of school like his brother. At the end of his teens, he left his father and went to the capital to work menial jobs like his brother. His two sisters got married without finishing their education as well. Their husbands were in a similar situation as Steve's brothers. Of course there was no real difference between their life after marriage and their life before.

Every individual in the family was responsible for themselves so Steve seized the opportunity to improve his and his family's situation and to take them out of the deprivation they had been living in. He struggled to save money to make the house habitable for any human. He rebuilt the house out of cement instead of mud. He also placed real furniture. He realized the different mindsets, between his and his parents. Not only because of the difference in age and education but also their acceptance of the situation as fact and their making no attempt to change. His parents were used to poverty and their way of living. They believed there was no harm to them to continue living in their poverty. Even receiving the basic necessities of life was too much of a task for them. Despite all this, they were not complaining or grumbling but had the belief that they were better off than most people. Because of their living situation, difficulty and lacking the necessities of life have been engrained in them. Even after living with Steve in an improved situation, increased income, and less mouths begging for food.

Steven started to bring home food from which they were previously derived. He started to bring beef. Beef was only associated with special events or during the harvest. A crisis would be if the grounds did not reap harvest and was a sign of increased level of incoming poverty. His parents were hard working farmers, and knew only how to work land. They had a very small piece of land and placed all their efforts into that land. Farmers spend so much time and effort on the land that they become one with the land and the land becomes visible on their faces. They became one with the land such that their harsh features resembled the rough ground they worked on, The land nor Steve's family had control over the land's affairs because the irrigation water was controlled by the government who opens the canals at will. The government also decides the type of crops and when to harvest, all of which are and is a very strict law. Because of this it's engraved in their mindset that they are unable to change their destiny.

One weekend, Steve came back from work looking forward to a hearty meal at home. He noticed that there was some meat in the fridge he had recently put there. He knows his mother was careful to prepare good meals on the weekend. He entered the house and sat on the sofa which he also put in recently to get some rest, since he had ridden his bike about six miles round trip on gravel road. He relaxed on the sofa and closed his eyes and deeply inhaled only to enter the smell of the hot soup his mother had prepared. Immediately, he went to wash up and change into comfortable clothes. While he was doing that, his mother prepared the food for him. The food was very delicious, as his mother was a good cook. So he ate until he was full and drank the soup until his stomach hurt. He ate the beef and felt it was too much. After he washed his hands he sat comfortably on the couch with his feet up. He thanked God for all that He had given him to change his family's life.

Suddenly he asked his mother about his spoiled cat, as he had not seen it since he entered the house. The cat did not purr up against his leg as he was eating, asking for food. His mother did not answer; he assumed she did not hear. Steven stood up looking for the cat. During his search he found the cat's skin in one of the house's corner, with some salt on it. Looked with panic at his mother. He went to the pot that they had just eaten dinner from.... "Whoa". Steven was infuriated and confused, up to the point of was going crazy. He asked his mother while he was pointing to the cat's skin "did I eat from it?' She nodded. He ran quickly to the fridge and found the meat that he had purchased in the fridge as it was.

The world had turned upside down. Steven did not know what to do with his parents; they had been used to eating kittens for a while. When he was young he would see them skin cats and his mother would cook it for them to eat. Even if it was kitten meat it was good and useful for their bodies. Their society was convinced it was good for the human from time to time to eat kitten meat. But Steven never participated in those meals. Many times he had eaten without knowing the source of the meat. To the point he was no longer able to differentiate between beef and the kitten meat.

Steven went to the pot on the stove and threw it on the ground. He went to the fridge and threw out all the food yelling "There is beef in the fridge! Why? Why?" He relived in his head how they would slaughter the cat and skin it in front of him and his siblings. He associated these images to their poverty. If they had a pound or two of beef his parents would never do this, But now, why? This question confused Steve a lot. Why are they now doing that when they know that God had blessed them and brought them out of severe poverty. Why, after he was able to fulfill all their basic needs and took his family out of poverty. The worst part was that this cat had a special place in Steve's heart? The cat had grown up with him.

Steven spent about ten days not eating or drinking anything in an attempt to forget what happened. He was unable to continue eating outside of home because the food was not good and the cost was high. Even the water he would drink from the water ways, he would not drink at home.

His father wondered why his son didn't like kitten meat. The kitten meat was not bad, thought his father.

Would you like to try my beloved reader? Please tell me after your first trial, and tell Steven's father.

Give me the Tithe

Peter was a young man in his last year of high school. When you sat with him, it is easy to recognize that his mental age exceeded his physical age. Even his spiritual stature preceded his age. Although he was slim and short with high cheek bones, he was not especially striking. But he displayed a depth in his life, which gave him a strong personality and veneration in his speech. He was also very emotional and highly sensitive which made him feel responsible for everyone, especially needy people.

Peter was responsible for managing the house. After the death of his father, he became responsible for collecting his father's retirement and care for the house, since the family had no other source of income. Peter learned from this responsibility; how God took care of his financial needs, even the trivial ones.

At the beginning of every month, when Peter collected retirement, he took out the tithe and gave it to the needy people. The rest he distributed among the necessities of the house. Nothing remained to be saved. Many times there would be a crisis, especially during Christmas and Easter because during those times it was customary to purchase clothes, sweets, and gifts. When the needs exceeded the income, somehow it was taken care of. The month of December was about to conclude and they were getting closer to Christmas. Peter had to provide all the Christmas needs for his family. However, much Peter's family was in need, he never took from his tithe. This was a source of argument between him and his mother. His mother would say that his family was in need just as much as the people to whom he gave tithes. He would quote the bible and say. *"Bring all the tithes into the storehouse that there may be food in My house, and try Me now in this, Says the Lord of hosts, If I will not open for you the windows of heaven and pour out for you such blessing that there will not be room enough to receive it."(Malachi 3:10)*

More often, she tried to discourage him from giving tithes especially during the Christmas and Easter time. Finally, when their arguments could not reach a conclusion, she disqualified Peter as the financial manager of the house. One or two months later, she gave him the rudder again. She wondered how he was able to manage their money to the end of the month and still pay tithes. Sometimes she borrowed to make ends meet. When she gave the responsibility back, Peter was responsible for paying the debts back.

Peter's mother brought him a paper with all of the Christmas needs. He took it from her, folded it, and put it in his pocket. As usual he said, "God will provide." With full faith he put these needs in his prayers.

George worked at the church as a custodian and loved Peter very much. The feeling was mutual. Many times Peter brought him gifts but Peter never knew the depth of George's poverty and Peter would never ask. On a Saturday evening, George asked Peter if he could help him with some clothes for his kids with any amount of money as George was really in need during the Christmas time. When George asked, he was ashamed and Peter felt the urgency of George's needs, as he had known him for long time, and many Christmases had passed and he never asked for anything. Peter felt that because there was love and affection between him and George, that George was able to ask when he was faced with difficulty. Peter promised he will do his best to fulfill George's request.

Peter entered the prayer meeting inside the church, but he could not pray at all. He remembered he used all the tithe money. What was remaining from the retirement money was hardly enough for their needs because he had needed the money for Christmas needs. He prayed to God to guide him in this financial dilemma. He couldn't stay in the church so he left the prayer meeting to go home.

On his way back home, he remembered that there was a piece of cloth from last year that no one used. When he asked his mother about the cloth he found out that the cloth had not yet been tailored. He asked his mother to get the cloth because he wanted to give it to one of the needy people. He felt his mother's resentment. But because she knew he would bring new cloth this year, she gave it to him. Peter took the cloth and withdrew ten pounds, went to the church and gave them to George. George thanked him, as he did not expect Peter's response to be so quick.

When Peter sat alone with himself in his room, praying, Peter contemplated how to obtain all the Christmas needs with the new budget and what else he was going to reduce. For a moment, Peter felt that he had made a mistake and that his family was right. He was conflicted and thought that just as he was not supposed to infringe on the tithe, he was also not supposed to infringe on the house's needs. He was supposed to give everyone their right. The piece of clothing was enough for George without the ten pounds. Peter felt remorse.

What hurt most was how was he going to tell his mother about the things he was going to reduce for Christmas. Peter thought, *what excuse was he going to offer her? He* knew very well the remaining money was barely enough for the most important needs.

Peter tried to study. He sat down more than an hour without turning the page. He took out the paper his mother gave him for the Christmas requirements. In the past week, Peter had been looking for cheap clothes for his brothers. What he bought was high quality cheap cloth.

His mother entered his room with a cup of tea and put it beside him and asked, "When will you go to buy the rest of the clothes for the Christmas and the rest of our needs?"

He answered her with vigor, "I will go."

She asked him again, "Is there anything you want to tell me?"

He answered "No." and looked down.

She came closer to him lifted his head from his chin with her right hand, looked him in the eye, and asked with tenderness, "What's wrong?"

Peter could not bear it. With shame he answered, "I have to reduce more from the Christmas needs."

She asked in a quiet tone "Why?"

"I gave ten pounds from the remaining money to a needy man that asked for help."

His mother fell silent for a moment and her face suddenly changed. She went to the reception yelling, calling her brothers, "Look what your brother did for you. He took your Christmas money and gave it to the poor." She started recalling all the things Peter had done and blamed him harshly in front of his brothers. She started mocking him, "Maybe you will sell the house furniture." From the intensity of her suffering she broke down in tears while saying, "Why Peter? Why? You know everything."

Peter could not bear his mother's tears nor his brothers' blaming stares. He went to his room and closed the door, and started weeping. As he felt he was guilty for what he did to his brothers. He tried to calm himself, but in vain. After couple of hours he went to his desk put his head between his hands and started to count the remaining money to figure out how he was going to deal with this situation.

From habit, Peter kept a good record of all the house expenses in a special notebook so he can keep track of the money. Peter was surprised; the money was the same since the last time he counted. He thought, because of his exhaustion, he must have miscounted. So he counted again. But he found the money did not detract from him. He took out the notebook he kept for finances, added the ten pounds he gave to Mr. George, and recalculated how much he should have. He found that the ten pounds had not been reduced. Peter could not believe himself; he knew this was a miracle. Peter believes in God's promises but this was the first time this had happened to him. He put the notebook and money aside. He raised his tear-filled eyes. But they were not like the previous tears. These were tears of thanks and happiness.

He called his mother and told her what happened. She said, "Are you trying to calm me down?" He tried to confirm with her what happened. He gave her the notebook and remaining money and asked her to review the money herself but she pushed his hand away while saying, "Do what you want," and she left without believing him or caring.

But Peter was very sure that what happened was a miracle by all means. As the lord says, *"Bring all the tithes into the storehouse that there may be food in My house, and try Me now in this, Says the Lord of hosts, If I will not open for you the windows of heaven and pour out for you such blessing that there will not be room enough to receive it.(Malachi 3:10) "*

The First and the Last

This story is not a love story; it is a story about love, a different kind of love. Love that can change a person from the bottom of disgrace to the top of virtue. Love that does not take from you, but gives. Love that pulls you out when you get drunk by the sinful cup. Not a love of flesh, *Eros*, but it is a divine love *Agape*. Love that burns your heart and allows you to willingly leave the wide sinful path. Love that makes you satisfied and happy with a new relationship.

The story you are about to embark on stresses God's continuous work in every person that honestly asks to know Him. God is able to visit any person regardless of his sin even if he is persecuting Him. This story shows us those people that thirst and hunger for the true life and look with all their hearts for the source of satisfaction. This story demonstrates how God can change a person, not to simply know Him and change their ways but to carry their cross every day and become an evangelist--to consecrate their life for the One that saved them. This story shows how the first can be last and the last can be first. As Jesus said "*But many who are first will be last, and the last first (Matthew19:30).*"

Joseph had just graduated from high school from one of the southern cities of Egypt and left his hometown to study dentistry in Cairo. He was the youngest among his brothers and all his brothers and sister did the same. They graduated from medical school without any problems. Upon arriving to the capital city, Joseph began living as he wanted. Being previously spoiled, now away from parental control, he accompanied himself with bad companions. Joseph began to spend many late nights. Joseph did not confine to give himself what he desired. As a natural result of his new lifestyle, he went from the top of his education to failing his courses, repeating many of them twice and sometimes even three times to pass. Joseph's family was well off but his material needs were endless. To his parents, his excuse was that he does not know how to cook and he always had to eat out so he could study.

Joseph got used to eating at a certain restaurant by his house. A beautiful young lady that had not finished her education was working at the restaurant. This woman, Sally used to work for her father's restaurant but left because of her stepmother, who had just borne a son from Sally's father. After her half-brother, Mohammad, was born, Sally could no longer live under the same roof and she could not bear the way her stepmother was dealing with her. Sally then left the house and the restaurant and went to go work for one of her father's friend's restaurant. Her father got busy with his new son and he stopped asking about his daughter.

Sally was looking for love, a warm love she did not have at home. She felt that all her male friends, coworkers, and regular guests only had one thing on their mind -- her body. Because of this, she hated men but as much as she hated them, she still had a need for a companion to give her the love she was looking for. She was not looking for a sexual relationship, but more of an intimate relationship. Joseph was a regular in the restaurant Sally worked at.

Joseph was tall, muscular, had broad shoulders, was tan, and had straight hair with dark blue eyes. Upon first impression, one would be deceived into thinking he was innocent but he was very far from it.

When Sally noticed he came regularly, she intended to make conversation with him. She knew he lived away from his family and he was studying dentistry in his second year but he did not ask her about anything. He felt as though t she was ineligible to even look at him, even if she, too, was attractive. Additionally, he had been attracted to another girl -- his schoolmate.

Joseph intentionally ignored her so he could see how far her feelings would go. As much as Joseph ignored her, she tried to promote courtship and emphasize her charms. They met outside the restaurant. She declared to him all her pain. How she grew up without her mother, how her stepmother treated her badly, how her father neglected her after her half-brother was born and how men harassed her. Joseph listened to her without uttering a word until she finished. He gave her an unexpected dose of sympathy. He told her she could consider him a big brother and she could count on him in anything she needed. He said that not as a caring man, but in order to get her trust. Joseph had other plans for her.

One day, Joseph asked her to bring dinner to his house and he knew that he would be alone. Even though she knew that he was alone, she still went. Upon her arrival, Joseph kissed Sally and hugged her warmly. It was not Joseph's first kiss. He had kissed many women before, but it was the first for Sally. Sally felt a tingling sensation and she began to want more than a kiss from him, which is exactly what Joseph was planning for.

They met several times in Joseph's apartment and it had become a completely sexual relationship. She started to spend nights with him and gradually she started to live with him. They lived in a mutually beneficial relationship, Joseph got laundry, a clean apartment, food, and sex and

Sally got the relationship she so desperately needed. She suspected that she was in a loving relationship with Joseph.

After a few months, Sally began to feel a large emptiness in her life, even thought she had everything she thought she needed. She's was looking for a kind of satisfaction she was not finding with her relationship with Joseph. He would leave her most of the day in his apartment and come in the evening. One day, while she was cleaning the apartment she found the Bible among Joseph's books which he never opened.. Out of curiosity, she opened it and started to read. As an unreligious Muslim woman, what she was reading was strange to her. She had never read something like this before. What she read gave comfort, a comfort she had been searching for a long time. What she read were simple words that touched her heart without complications. These words translated to a great love for a greater God that saved the world as a result of His love.

The meaning of salvation was completely new to her. She did not comprehend it well enough; however she was in deep need for this salvation. The Bible, especially the New Testament, had become her only friend in her loneliness, especially after she stopped working and moved in with Joseph. She was reading *"For God so loved the world that He gave His only begotten Son, that whoever believes in Him should not perish but have everlasting life."(John 3:16) "Take My yoke upon you and learn from Me, for I am gentle and lowly in heart, and you will find rest for your souls. 30 For My yoke is easy and My burden is light" (Matthew11:29)*. She began reading eagerly and insatiably.

Joseph noticed some changes with Sally. She stopped sleeping with him and gave him many excuses and she stopped responding to his flirtations. He was curious as to what caused the change, but he never expected that she would be reading the bible.

One night Joseph came back to find Sally exhausted from weeping and crying. He was shocked and asked if she had heard bad news, but she shook her head. Suddenly she said to him, "Tell me about Jesus. I want to become a Christian." It was a complete shock to Joseph. He did not utter a word and he stared at her in awe. That was the last thing he ever expected to happen. Even though he was Christian, he never told her about Christianity and he never acted as a Christian his entire life. He never read the Bible or went to church. He swallowed hard saying, "Are you crazy?"

"Where is the craziness in what I asked you?"

Joseph sat beside her and asked her, "From where did you get this idea?"

She took out the Bible and handed it to him and said, "This is the reason."

He put his hand on her cheek and said, "This will cause a lot of trouble, and maybe your family will kill..."

She cut him off, leapt up from his side, angrily swiped his hand off her face and said, "Whatever will happen, and you have to know from now on, you will never touch me until I become Christian and we get married, other than that, this is impossible."

Her words hit Joseph like a thunderbolt. He was not able to understand why and how she was able to change. She continued saying, "How can you have such satisfying words in the bible, and you live your life like this in sin. Maybe I have an excuse, because in my religion I did not find this love and satisfaction, even if I was not that religious, I have never found before what I have found in the Bible."

"Since when have you been reading the bible?" Joseph asked.

"A few months."

After a moment of silence from Joseph, he said, "Listen, I do not want any problems, if you want to become a Christian that is your decision. I will show you one of the nearest churches and you can go to the father. You can do whatever you want but do not involve me in anything."

Joseph prepared his dinner and when he went to sleep he found the bedroom door was locked, he tried to get her to open it, but in vain. He spent the night on the couch. Two days later, when Joseph came back home she was not there. When he looked for her, he knew that she went to the priest he told her about. Joseph was very surprised from this change that happened to Sally.

How could a girl like Sally change so dramatically when she did not grow in a strong, united house, but a divided one? She did not know anything about her religion. In his eyes, she was a lustful woman. No one told her about Christianity, so how did she come to know the Bible? How does she love Christianity? How can one like her understand what it is to be a Christian?

Religion for Joseph was just something inherited from his family, but for him it was not a belief. He could be any other religion if he was born into a different family. He never tried to ask himself why he was a Christian and what it meant to be a Christian. He knew that Jesus came to the world, was born of the Virgin, lived like us, and was crucified, resurrected, and ascended to heaven. That was all he knew about Christianity, he never tried one day to know more. He just lived like most of the people. Religion to him was just a social thing. To be a good Christian and to know the faith he had to go to the church, and that was something he just did not do. He got bored from the priest's words and he did not like to pray. What did Sally find in the Bible that could change her way of thinking?

Since his middle school years, he stopped reading the Bible and did not care to understand more about it.. He felt that he was not in need of understanding so he put the Bible aside.

How did Sally understand and how did that understanding lead to her conversion? This made Joseph astonished and confused.

A few days later, Joseph went to the church to meet his friends. While he was there, the priest asked to see him. The father started to ask him how he knew Sally, how long he had known her and how he met her. So Joseph started to tell him everything. When Joseph started asking the father about where she was or what she was going to do, the father did not answer. He recommended that he not tell anybody about her and if somebody asked, his answer should be "I don't know."

Joseph begged the priest to keep him out of any trouble and to not impose his name in anything. The father patted his shoulder, promised him, and dismissed him.

After a few weeks, Joseph started to forget everything about Sally and what happened. He was surprised when one of his friends told him that Sally had been baptized and became a Christian, and that the father was trying to send her out of the country to be safe. When Joseph sat by himself, he thought how he could get the most benefit out of this situation as he always does. Why doesn't he travel with her? If she wants to marry him, no problem. For sure, she will need someone in the foreign country to help her. Especially if it is someone she already knows. He had always dreamt of living in a foreign country, like most people in Egypt and the chance was at hand, he couldn't lose it.

Joseph went to the priest and asked about Sally. He appeared happy because she had become a Christian. He told the priest that he loved her and that he wanted to get married and travel with her to any European country. When Sally found out, she did not mind, especially since she still had feelings for Joseph. But she still didn't trust him.

She met him after a long time and Joseph found that Sally had completely changed physically, in her behavior, and her way of speaking. He did not recognize the secret behind her becoming a Christian and now she was full of the blessing and had been baptized and obtained the Eucharist. She had become more pretty with no comparison to her before. That made Joseph seriously think about marrying her.

They got married. A few days later they left to one of the European countries. Joseph did not tell his family anything. He only told them that he was leaving.

Joseph was not able to carry the responsibility of a married man. He wanted her to be with him as he was before. He was not able to withstand her strict religious way of living. She was going to church, praying, fasting, and reading the Bible constantly. She wanted to live the true life of Christianity.

Joseph eventually went back to his sinful ways with the blonde women of Europe. Sally, unable to bear the situation, separated from him for his unfaithfulness. She went to a nunnery and consecrated her life to serve the sick and elderly people. Joseph plunged in the sinful life and he got the citizenship. Whenever he remembers her he would ask himself, "How did she become like this? What did she find in Christianity to believe in?" He never knew the answer to this question, and I think he will never know the answer. But Sally is still praying for him to change, repent, and to become a true Christian like her.

Truly as Jesus said, *"who are first will be last, and the last first (Matthew19:30)."*

Unless You Marry Me

Hanna was in her late thirties and not yet married. She was a simple woman, not gorgeous, but not unattractive either. There were many women less attractive or equal and they were able to get married long before. All the circumstances that Hanna endured in her life contributed a great deal to her single status.

Hanna's father passed away when she was a teenager. She had no siblings. She lived with her mother in a small studio, in one of the poorest neighborhoods in the outskirts of the city but looked more like a village. You would see animals and their feces in the alleys.

Hanna had not finished her education, not because she was unintelligent or she failed, but because of the necessity of money in her family life. Her mother was not convinced it was important for her to finish her education, and thought that one day Hanna would get married and all her attention would be for the house and kids. Their only source of income was the pension which was about a hundred pounds. The church also helped a bit by providing small donations.

Hanna has some innate intelligence as well as an effervescent personality. She gestured a lot while making a point. Hanna started to become naturally aware that she was at the critical age to get married. Until then, no one had asked for her hand_in marriage. However as much as she tried to socialize at the church, it was all in vain. After church events, she would stand alone because she had nothing in common with the people and she would leave reluctantly. Gradually, she stopped going to church. As a result, the servants started asking about her. They got used to her absence and she got used to not going. However, she still went once a month to get the monthly assistance. She would also go during Christmas and Easter to get the donation in kind after her mother's pleas.

Hanna prepared bread at home and when she or her mother was sick or there was no flour at home, she would go to the bakery to buy bread instead. She started to go to the bakery regularly because her mother was sick. The baker started to become interested in her. He started to stare at her for a long time. When she did not respond, he started to flirt openly; maybe he could attract her with his words.

After a while, the baker succeeded in attracting her attention. After she went home from the bakery, she started to think of him as a man. She started to deliberately not make bread at home, creating many excuses to go to the bakery. Instead of buying bread for two, three days ahead, she would buy daily and her excuse was to buy fresh bread every day. Her mother did not recognize the change in her daughter. She began to spend more time outside when she was previously fairly sedentary. The baker, unlike the rest of men provoked Hanna's femininity, which was neglected for a long time.

One night Hanna went in a hurry from her house because she had a date with the baker who claimed he needed her for a serious matter. They met in a junkyard next to one of the canals. While holding her hand, he told her he could not bear it anymore and he wanted to marry her. She pulled her hand quickly saying, "Marry me? How and you are..."

"I am what? I am a Muslim and you are Christian. What is the problem with that? We will marry and everyone will remain in their religion. For the children fifty-fifty, the boys follow my faith and the girls yours. Unless you want to become a Muslim."

"Impossible."

"Well, we will marry and everyone remains in their religion." Hanna looked at the ground and he continued "I will prepare everything." Hanna pulled herself from him and went back home to find her mother home, worrying about her because she was not used to Hanna coming home late.

Her face was changed and she was engrossed in thought. Her mother never knew the cause beyond this change and of course Hanna did not tell her anything. Hanna wondered, *"There is no one else but this man, this man of a different religion, who wants to marry me? Why is there no Christian man that wants to marry me? I want to be a wife and a mother but not in this way. After a while my mother will pass away and I will be lonely, and what will I do after that. There is no one asking about me now, how will it be after my mother passes away. I don't want to live alone. It does not look like there is someone that will think of marrying me if I wait more, and this man does not ask me to change my religion. He is not forcing me to do so. I can marry him and remain Christian. This is too hard for me and I don't like it. I wouldn't like to marry someone a different religion from me. But what is it that I got from my religion? My simple needs as a woman I can't get.*

Although her meeting with the baker was late at night, in a junkyard, and no one accompanied or heard them, but the next day Hanna was surprised that everyone knew. While walking in the ally many hinted that they knew of her relationship and the signs of disgust were on the Christians' face. No one was speaking openly about this topic_ because of this she was comforted. Her mother knew nothing about what was going on, even though it was rumored by everyone.

Mr. Samuel was elderly, but also large. Everything about him was huge. He had a huge structure, huge ears, huge nose, and huge lips.

His eyes were wide. Walking with him you felt you were walking with a body builder. He was old to the ministry in this area and he was one of the oldest fathers of the ministry where Hanna lived. Many times he visited the people in the area including Hanna's house and he knew them by name. He recommended that the servants visit the area especially Hanna and her mother. But none of the servants took action. The servants started to blame her claiming that, "This is where she was expected to end up." Mr. Samuel brought one of the new servants, John that recently graduated from the college to visit Hanna, after they heard about her relationship with the baker and what she intended to do.

Mr. Samuel knocked on the door, Hanna opened. At first glance she was surprised because a long time had passed and he did not visit. But she knew inside her why he came to visit her. She asked him to come in. Mr. Samuel initiated the conversation by asking about her, her mother, if she is getting the monthly help on time, and why she stopped going to church lately. Her answers were typical. After a moment of silence Mr. Samuel asked her, "Is it true what we have heard about you Hanna?"

She answered in craftiness "What exactly have you heard?"

Mr. Samuel sighed and he recognized she was being crafty and defending herself. So he said to her while pulling out the Bible from his pocket without looking at her, "Your relationship with the baker."

She answered surprisingly, "Relationship? There is nothing between me and him!"

Mr. Samuel looked at her and wondered how she was so bold. She put her hands on her stomach in a defensive position. So he asked her again, "What about marrying him?"

She answered nervously in a loud voice with radical movement from her right hand, "He asked me but I have not answered him yet."

"What is your answer?"

"No one else has asked to marry me!"

"That means you have agreed?"

Hanna kept silent and looked down. Mr. Samuel opened the bible to the second epistle of St. Paul to the Corinthians and he started reading, *"Do not be unequally yoked together with unbelievers. For what fellowship has righteousness with lawlessness? And what communion has light with darkness? And what accord has Christ with Belial? Or what part has a believer with an unbeliever? "* *(2Cori6:14-15).* After he finished, he started to explain to her, "Marriage is a sacrament and is a holy life. The two become one body in Christ and this is not available with a partner of different faith..."

Hanna cut him off, "What are you expecting me to do? No one else has asked my hand in marriage, and it is clear no one will because I am poor and unattractive. My mother will leave me very soon, what do you expect me to do? He has not asked me to change my faith."

John watched all of this without uttering a word. For him it was his first time to see this scene. He said in a calm voice addressed to Hanna, "Do you trust in Christ's promises? He said 'I will never leave or forsake you' even if a mother forgets her nursing baby, He will never forget you. If He is taking care of the birds in the sky and the lilies in the field will he not take care of you?"

Hanna looked at him wonderingly and asked herself, "From where did this man come?" She had not realized his presence. Her heated conversation with Mr. Samuel was so indulging that she did not notice John.. She looked at him from head to toe until John got shy from the way she was looking at him; he looked to Mr. Samuel questioning what she wants from him. Hanna started pointing at John saying, "Look at you, you are a handsome young man, very well education, from a good family, do you think you could look at one like me and ask for marriage? If you marry me, I won't marry the baker."

Ending the conversation she looked away. John blushed and a moment passed that felt like eternity. Mr. Samuel did not answer; he was waiting for the answer to come from John. John swallowed and he tried to answer, he explaining that they do not match and there are many other dimensions in marriage other than religion, like age, education, and social level. But he felt that she was not listening and he had not convinced her.

She asked him again, "Are you willing to do anything for Jesus?"

John nodded. Waiting for her to continue.

"Then, for His sake, marry me. Or…" She looked away.

Mr. Samuel stood up and grabbed John upward because he felt that there is futility to continue talking to her.

Mr. Samuel said to her, "Shame on you Hanna. Know that what you are doing is wrong, I am here to warn you." Then he left with John.

After a while the servants at the church heard that she married the baker and left her mother and went to live with him in another city. News of her ceased completely. No one knows if she remained with her faith. However news of Hanna ceased, there are many like her. Every one of them has a story not much different than hers. The confusing question will remain, who is responsible for Hanna leaving Christ. Her circumstances, the servants neglecting her, no one considered Hanna for marriage, or is the complete responsibility on Hanna. Whatever your opinion I want you to pray for Hanna and for many others like her in Egypt that were deceived by many to leave their faith and follow marriage.

Conclusion

My beloved reader, did you like the book? I think you did. My target from this book is not that you close it after reading, look at it and say, "Nice stories" and put it aside. If you will do so, I consider myself a failure in the purpose of this book. But, if these stories will increase your faith, and you remember it in your daily lives, and tell others about it, I will consider myself a partial success. If you will take the initiative to pray for these countries, tribes, and individuals I am a notch under success. If you feel responsibility towards this evangelism and you start to support it, I will consider myself very close. But what I am aiming for is that you become a missionary and evangelize the name of Jesus everywhere. If you cannot go to the end of the world, at least evangelize where you are. Be fruitful where God has planted you, Be Jesus' image which the world is in full need of now. Brush off negative dust from yourself and as a good soldier for Christ; carry the hardship for His sake. He wants to talk to his creation but he wants to do that through you because he never worked without man.

Stand up now and ask him, "Lord what do you want me to do to expand your kingdom, your love, on earth?" I am positive he will guide you. Be ready to do whatever he asks of you even if it is illogical from your perspective.

God bless you,
Isaac Akladeos
www.mission-forchrist.com

www.ingramcontent.com/pod-product-compliance
Lightning Source LLC
Chambersburg PA
CBHW031522040426
42445CB00009B/353